"TOWARD FULL COMMUNION" AND "CONCORDAT OF AGREEMENT"

*Lutheran–Episcopal
Dialogue, Series III*

Edited by
William A. Norgren
and William G. Rusch

Augsburg
Minneapolis

Forward Movement Publications
Cincinnati

"TOWARD FULL COMMUNION" AND "CONCORDAT OF AGREEMENT"
Lutheran–Episcopal Dialogue, Series III

Copyright © 1991 Augsburg Fortress

Published by Augsburg, 426 S. Fifth St., Box 1209, Minneapolis
MN 55440 and Forward Movement Publications, 412 Sycamore St.,
Cincinnati OH 45202.

Scripture quotations unless otherwise noted are from the Revised Standard Version
of the Bible, copyright © 1946, 1952, and 1971 by the Division of Christian Education
of the National Council of Churches.

Library of Congress Cataloging-in-Publication Data

Lutheran–Episcopal Dialogue (3rd : 1983–1991)
    "Toward full communion" and "Concordat of agreement" / Lutheran
–Episcopal Dialogue, series III ; edited by William A. Norgren and
William G. Rusch.
        p. cm.
    Includes bibliographical references.
    ISBN 0-8066-2578-3 (Augsburg) — ISBN 0-88028-119-7
(Forward Movement Publications)
        1. Episcopal Church—Relations—Evangelical Lutheran Church in
America—Congresses.   2. Evangelical Lutheran Church in America—
Relations—Episcopal Church—Congresses.   3. Episcopacy—
Congresses.   4. Christian union—Congresses.   5. Anglican
Communion—Relations—Lutheran Church—Congresses.   6. Lutheran
Church—Relations—Anglican Communion—Congresses.   I. Norgren,
William A.   II. Rusch, William G.   III. Title.
BX5928.5.E95L88   1991
284.1'332—dc20   91-12472
                                                                   CIP

Manufactured in the U.S.A.   AF 9-2578

95   94   93   92   91   1   2   3   4   5   6   7   8   9   10

Contents

3

CONCORDAT OF AGREEMENT

Preface

The Lutheran-Episcopal dialogue in the United States has been at work for more than twenty years and has resulted in a number of important reports. In 1982 the *Lutheran-Episcopal Agreement* held before the sponsoring churches the goal of full communion and presented a mandate for the third series of Lutheran-Episcopal dialogues. This mandate, supported by the Episcopal Church in the United States, the American Lutheran Church, the Association of Evangelical Lutheran Churches, and the Lutheran Church in America, called for discussion of implications of the gospel and the ordering of ministry (bishops, priests, and deacons) in the total context of apostolicity. It is clear from the mandate given to the dialogue that Lutherans wished greater assurance about consensus in the gospel, and Episcopalians greater clarity about order in the church before proceeding toward full communion.

The third series of Lutheran-Episcopal dialogues has respected this request from the churches. It first turned its attention in 1983 to the part of the mandate that focused on implications of the gospel. In 1988 it published the volume *Implications of the Gospel*; the sponsoring churches will consider formal action on this dialogue report in the summer of 1991.

Between 1988 and 1991 the dialogue devoted its energies to the question of ministry and order in the church. Now the dialogue has completed its work. This publication, *"Toward Full Communion" and "Concordat of Agreement,"* represents the completion of the work assigned to the dialogue by the churches. It is based on more than twenty years of international, regional, national, and local dialogue between Anglicans and Lutherans, and the insights of contemporary ecumenical theology. If the churches wish, the results of the third series of Lutheran-Episcopal dialogue can move them beyond the *Lutheran-Episcopal Agreement* of 1982 toward full communion. The dialogue's work is a call for recognition of both churches as fully *Church* united in mission and service.

Clearly one phase of the ongoing process of rapprochement has ended. The challenge before the Episcopal Church in the United States and the Evangelical Lutheran Church in America is one of careful study and evaluation of the work and recommendations of this dialogue. They are being challenged in the ecumenical sense of the term to engage in "reception." This will require some years for both churches and should not be done precipitously. They will need to consult with the Lutheran and Anglican communions internationally and with other ecumenical partners. The work of this series of dialogues offers possibilities to these two churches, and to all churches committed to the ecumenical movement, to move beyond their present separation and disunity toward full communion, but not structural merger. It is in this spirit that the dialogue offers its work to the churches.

Toward Full Communion begins by tracing the work of the dialogue until 1991. The first chapter describes the historic impasse between Lutherans and Anglicans on ministry, and especially the historic episcopate, and indicates resources to break this impasse. Chapter 2 presents the theological consensus between Anglicans and Lutherans identified through decades of dialogue. Chapters 3 and 4 are concerned with Lutheran churches and episcopal ministry and the Episcopal Church and the ministry of the historic episcopate. The last chapter addresses the gift of full communion.

The Concordat of Agreement describes the basis and several actions of each church that would bring them into full communion. An agreement in the doctrine of the faith leads to recognition and interchangeability of ministers and members, joint consecrations of future bishops, and the establishment of organs for consultation and communication to express and strengthen fellowship and to enable common witness, life and service.

This volume also includes *The Dissenting Report*, *The Assenting Report*, and the *Statement of Lutheran Church—Missouri Synod Participants*.

We commend the following pages to our churches for careful evaluation with the hope that they will find in them a resource to express more faithfully to the world around them that unity in being and mission which we believe the Lord of the church has willed for Christ's people.

William A. Norgren
Ecumenical Officer
The Episcopal Church

William G. Rusch
Executive Director
Office for Ecumenical Affairs
Evangelical Lutheran Church
in America

Week of Prayer for Christian Unity — 1991

Toward Full Communion

Between

the Episcopal Church and

the Evangelical Lutheran Church in America

Introduction

1.   Bilateral dialogue between the Episcopal Church in the U.S.A. and the Lutheran churches which were members of the Lutheran Council in the U.S.A. at that time (The American Lutheran Church, The Lutheran Church in America, and The Lutheran Church—Missouri Synod) was authorized in 1967. The conversations began on October 14, 1969. The first round of conversations (LED I) concluded on June 1, 1972. The agreements, recommendations, and papers were published at the end of 1972 under the title *Lutheran-Episcopal Dialogue: A Progress Report.* The recommendations included "continuing joint theological study and conversation."[1] A second round of conversations (LED II) began in January, 1976, and concluded in November, 1980. The proceedings were published in 1981 under the title *Lutheran-Episcopal Dialogue: Report and Recommendations.*[2] In September of 1978 a representative of the Association of Evangelical Lutheran Churches joined the dialogue. In September, 1982, the Episcopal Church and three of the Lutheran churches, the American Lutheran Church, the Association of Evangelical Lutheran Churches, and the Lutheran Church in America, approved the Lutheran-Episcopal Agreement as follows:

The Episcopal Church and the Lutheran Churches

1) Welcome and rejoice in the substantial progress of the Lutheran-Episcopal Dialogues (LED) I and II and of the Anglican-Lutheran International Conversations, looking forward to the day when full communion is established between the Anglican and Lutheran Churches;

2) Recognize now the (Episcopal Church/The American Lutheran Church, Lutheran Church in America, Association of Evangelical Lutheran Churches) as Churches in which the Gospel is preached and taught;

3) Encourage the development of common Christian life throughout the respective Churches by such means as the following:

11

a) Mutual prayer and mutual support, including parochial/congregational and diocesan/synodical covenants or agreements,
b) Common study of the Holy Scriptures, the histories and theological traditions of each Church, and the material of LED I and II,
c) Joint programs of religious education, theological discussion, mission, evangelism, and social action,
d) Joint use of facilities;

4) Affirm now on the basis of studies of LED I and LED II and of the Anglican/Lutheran International Conversations that the basic teaching of each respective Church is consonant with the Gospel and is sufficiently compatible with the teaching of this Church that a relationship of Interim Sharing of the Eucharist is hereby established between these Churches in the U.S.A. under the following guidelines:
a) The Episcopal Church extends a special welcome to members of these three Lutheran Churches to receive Holy Communion in it under the Standard for Occasional Eucharist Sharing of its 1979 General Convention.
or   (The Lutheran Churches) Extend a special welcome to members of the Episcopal Church to receive Holy Communion in it under the Statement on Communion Practices adopted in 1978.
This welcome constitutes a mutual recognition of Eucharistic teaching sufficient for Interim Sharing of the Eucharist, although this does not intend to signify that final recognition of each other's Eucharists or ministries has yet been achieved.
b) Bishops of Dioceses of the Episcopal Church and Bishops/Presidents of the Lutheran Districts and Synods may by mutual agreement extend the regulations of Church discipline to permit common, joint celebrations of the Eucharist within their jurisdictions.   This is appropriate in particular situations where the said authorities deem that local conditions are appropriate for the sharing of worship jointly by congregations of the respective Churches. The presence of an ordained minister of each participating Church at the altar in this way reflects the presence of two or more Churches expressing unity in faith and baptism as well as the remaining divisions which they seek to overcome; however, this does not imply rejection or final recognition of either Church's Eucharist or ministry. In such circumstances the eucharistic prayer will be one from the *Lutheran Book of Worship* or the *Book of Common Prayer* as authorized jointly by the Bishop of the Episcopal Diocese and the Bishops/Presidents of the corresponding Lutheran Districts/Synods.
c) This resolution and experience of Interim Sharing of the Eucharist will be communicated at regular intervals to other Churches of the Lutheran and Anglican Communions throughout the world, as well

12

as to the various ecumenical dialogues in which Anglicans and Lutherans are engaged, in order that consultation may be fostered, similar experiences encouraged elsewhere, and already existing relationships of full communion respected;

5) Authorize and establish now a third series of Lutheran-Episcopal Dialogues for the discussion of any other outstanding questions that must be resolved before full communion (*communio in sacris*/altar and pulpit fellowship) can be established between the respective Churches, e.g., implications of the Gospel, historic episcopate, and the ordering of ministry (Bishops, Priests, and Deacons) in the total context of apostolicity.[3]

2.   Lutherans and Anglicans have been in official conversation since the late nineteenth century.[4] In 1909, the Lambeth Conference, representing in some sense the entire Anglican Communion, and with one American bishop on its committee, began dialogue with the Church of Sweden.[5] Before the onset of World War II the conversation had expanded to include the Churches of Finland, Estonia, and Latvia. In 1947 the conversations expanded again to include the Churches of Norway, Denmark, and Iceland. The gift of unity disclosed and discovered in these early conversations resulted in a significant expansion of contacts and agreements which specified an important degree of intercommunion. The first official conversation in this century involving Anglicans and Lutherans in the U.S.A. took place in December, 1935, between The Episcopal Church and The Augustana Evangelical Lutheran Church, a church with its roots in Sweden. The antipathy of the Lutherans to the historic episcopate as it was then perceived and sometimes advocated as well as commitment to growing unity among Lutherans led to a termination of the official conversation after one meeting, although "the colloquy called for the continuation of its efforts and adjourned in a friendly spirit."[6]

3.   The Lutheran-Episcopal Agreement of 1982 advances the relationship between churches of the Lutheran and Anglican communions because it involves churches who live side by side in the same country. These churches have come to a new stage in their relationship, a stage characterized by the phrase, "Interim Sharing of the Eucharist." Christ Jesus, Our Lord, gives to the church the gifts of ministry for building up his body toward maturity and wholeness (Eph. 4:11-16). Every level of maturity which is expressed by Christian unity is occasion for thanksgiving. Lutherans and Episcopalians are grateful to God not only for the Agreement of 1982, but also, and

above all, for the reception of that agreement by the churches. Throughout the U.S.A., Episcopalians and Lutherans have been experiencing in worship and study, in covenants and cooperation, a growing common life and apostolic mission.

4.   Now a third series of dialogues (LED III) has been under way since 1983. In response to the mandate from our churches to address such "outstanding questions" as "implications of the Gospel," LED III has published *Implications of the Gospel*[7] in 1988. This document was commended to both churches by their respective standing committees charged with responsibility for ecumenical affairs. The 1988 General Convention of the Episcopal Church and the 1989 Assembly of the Evangelical Lutheran Church in America encouraged its study by clergy and parishes for report back in 1991 as a contribution to the larger effort of moving toward full communion. Its comprehensive character demonstrates the breadth of theological consensus which exists between our traditions. *Implications of the Gospel*, together with its study guide, also provides theological resources for "joint programs of religious education, theological discussion, mission, evangelism and social action" encouraged in provision 3c of the 1982 Agreement.

5.   The goal of LED III, mandated by our churches in 1982, is "full communion." In addition to agreement on *Implications of the Gospel*, the action of 1982 requires attention to the "historic episcopate, and the ordering of ministry (Bishops, Priests, and Deacons) in the total context of apostolicity." Subsequent to the mandate of 1982, the term "full communion" is used to identify the ecumenical goal in reports and actions of the Anglican Consultative Council and the Lutheran World Federation as well as in the working document on ecumenism adopted by the Evangelical Lutheran Church in America in 1989. We cite the following actions and documents as examples of this usage.

a. In the Lutheran World Federation, "The *Executive Committee*, with its Standing Committee on Ecumenical Relations (established 1972), is responsible for the interconfessional dialogs and ecumenical relations."[8] In 1983 the Executive Committee of the Lutheran World Federation and the Anglican Consultative Council convened an Anglican-Lutheran "Joint Working Group" at Cold Ash, England. In its report, this "Joint Working Group" described the then current state of Anglican-Lutheran relationships and formulated a statement on the "Goal of Anglican-

Lutheran Dialogue." In 1984 the General Secretary of the Lutheran World Federation reported to the Assembly that the Executive Committee received the Cold Ash Report which "stated the goal of the Anglican-Lutheran dialog: 'We look forward to the day when full communion is established between Anglican and Lutheran churches.'"[9] It "voted to establish a joint Anglican/Lutheran committee, as suggested in the report."[10] At Budapest, in 1984, the 7th Assembly of the Lutheran World Federation received a report which encouraged "member churches living in the same region as Anglican churches . . . to support the mutual direction toward church fellowship, and in their region to act together according to the recommendations of the international and regional consultations." The Assembly resolved "to recommend to the LWF Executive Committee that the dialogs with . . . the Anglican churches be conducted as planned, geared to the above-mentioned goals."[11]

b. The Anglican Consultative Council, meeting in 1984, commended the Cold Ash report "to the member Churches," and on its basis recommended "that Anglican Churches should officially encourage the practice of eucharistic hospitality to Lutherans," "that as a further step towards full communion . . . the churches should consider making provision for appropriate forms of 'interim eucharistic sharing' along the lines of that authorized in the U.S.A.," and endorsed "the proposals for closer collaboration between the ACC and the Lutheran World Federation" as set out in the report.[12]

c. The 1988 Lambeth Conference of the bishops of the Anglican Communion adopted a resolution which included the following provisions:

> 4 Recognizes, on the basis of the high degree of consensus reached in international, regional and national dialogues between Anglicans and Lutherans and in the light of the communion centered around Word and Sacrament that has been experienced in each other's traditions, the presence of the Church of Jesus Christ in the Lutheran Communion as in our own.
> 5 Urges that this recognition and the most recent convergence on apostolic ministry achieved in the *Niagara Report* on the Anglican-Lutheran Consultation on Episcopacy (1987) prompt us to move towards the fullest possible ecclesial recognition and the goal of full communion.[13]

d. The Executive Committee of the Lutheran World Federation, meeting in Geneva, Switzerland, July 31 to August 9, 1989, adopted unanimously a series of recommendations on Lutheran-Anglican relationships for action by the 1990 Assembly of the LWF, including the following:

> 7.1 that the LWF renew its commitment to the goal of full communion (see Report of the Anglican-Lutheran Joint Working Group - Cold Ash Report - 1983, paras. 25-27) with the churches of the Anglican Communion, and that it urge LWF member churches to take appropriate steps toward its realization;
> 7.2 that the LWF acknowledge with gratitude the 1988 Resolution on A-L relations of the Lambeth Conference and that it concur with that Conference's recommendations to Anglican and Lutheran churches;
> 7.3 that the LWF note with thanksgiving the steps toward church fellowship with national/regional Anglican counterparts which LWF member churches have been able to take already and that it encourage them to proceed;
> 7.4 that the Anglican-Lutheran International Commission both arrange for further global studies and reports which may be needed and that ALIC be prepared to assist Anglican and Lutheran churches in taking steps toward full communion.[14]

This recommendation was adopted by the 1990 assembly at Curitiba, Brazil.[15]

e. The 1989 Assembly of the Evangelical Lutheran Church in America adopted "Ecumenism: The Vision of the Evangelical Lutheran Church in America" as a "working document," which means that it is "to offer provisional and interim guidance for this church during the 1990-1991 biennium." The document states:

> D. *Goal and Stages of Relationships*
> The Evangelical Lutheran Church in America is an active participant in the ecumenical movement, because of its desire of Christian unity. Its goal is full communion, i.e. the full or complete realization of unity with all those churches that confess the Triune God. The Evangelical Lutheran Church in America, both as a church and as a member of the wider communion of churches in the Lutheran World Federation, seeks to reach this goal.
> Full communion will be a gift from God and will be founded on faith in Jesus Christ. It will be a commitment to truth in love and a witness to God's liberation and reconciliation. Full communion

16

will be visible and sacramental. It is obviously a goal toward which divided churches, under God's Spirit, are striving, but which has not been reached. It is also a goal in need of continuing definition. It will be rooted in agreement on essentials and allow diversity in nonessentials.

However, in most cases the churches will not be able to move immediately from their disunity to a full expression of their God-given unity, but can expect to experience a movement from disunity to unity that may include one or more of the following stages of relationships.

1. *Ecumenical Cooperation.* Here the Evangelical Lutheran Church in America enters into ecumenical relations based on the *evangelical* and *representative* principles.

2. *Bilateral and Multilateral Dialogues.* Here the Evangelical Lutheran Church in America enters into dialogues, with varying mandates, with those who agree with the evangelical and representative principles, confess the Triune God, and share a commitment to "ecumenical conversion." This conversion or repentance includes openness to new possibilities under the guidance of God's Spirit.

3. *Preliminary Recognition.* Here the Evangelical Lutheran Church in America can be involved on a church-to-church basis in eucharistic sharing and cooperation, without exchangeability of ministers.

a. One stage requires 1 and 2 above, plus partial, mutual recognition of church and sacraments with partial agreement in doctrine.

b. A second stage requires 1, 2, and 3a, partial and mutual recognition of ordained ministers and of churches, fuller agreement in doctrine, commitments to work for full communion, and preliminary agreement on lifting of any mutual condemnations.

4. *Full Communion.* At this stage the goal of the involvement of this church in the ecumenical movement has been fully attained. Here the question of the shape and form of full communion needs to be addressed and answered in terms of what will best further the mission of the Church in individual cases.

For the Evangelical Lutheran Church in America, the characteristics of full communion will include at least the following, some of which will exist at earlier stages:

1. a common confessing of the Christian faith;

2. a mutual recognition of Baptism and a sharing the Lord's Supper, allowing for an exchangeability of members;

3. a mutual recognition and availability of ordained ministers to the service of all members of churches in full communion, subject only but always to the disciplinary regulations of the other churches;

17

    4. a common commitment to evangelism, witness, and service;

    5. a means of common decision making on critical common issues of faith and life;

    6. a mutual lifting of any condemnations that exist between churches.

This definition of full communion is understood to be consistent with Article VII of the Augsburg Confession, which says, "for the true unity of the church it is enough to agree concerning the teaching of the Gospel and the administration of the sacraments." Agreement in the Gospel can be reached and stated without adopting Lutheran confessional formulations as such.[16]

6.   Both of our churches have recognized the gift of unity in the gospel (unity in the faith) which has been given to us. Both of our churches expect us to respond to that gift through our search for appropriate ecclesial structures by which we can give expression to that gift. In the Concordat of Agreement appended to this document we will make recommendations to our churches which will take us from the stage of "Interim Sharing of the Eucharist" to expressions of unity commensurate with the degree of consensus we have reached up to this point, stages which will reflect our growing ability to share ecclesial structures. Full communion will include full interchangeability and reciprocity of ordained ministries "subject only but always to the disciplinary regulations of the other churches,"[17] processes for consultation, shared involvement in mission, and agreement in decision making. Such expressions of communion are based on common understanding of the doctrine of the faith (confession of the gospel), mutual recognition of baptism, and sharing together in the eucharist. It is clear from the mandate given by both our churches that questions involved in the historic episcopate and the ordering of ministry will have to be resolved in order for our churches to be in full communion with each other.

1

The Historic Impasse

7.   We approach these issues of ministry in sober awareness of the importance and the difficulty of the task. Since the adoption of the Chicago-Lambeth Quadrilateral of 1886-88, the Episcopal Church has been committed to the principle that "the Historic Episcopate, locally adapted in the methods of its administration to the varying needs of the nations and peoples called of God into the Unity of His Church" is one of the four elements (together with the Holy Scriptures, the Apostles' and Nicene Creeds, and the sacraments of baptism and eucharist) that constitute the *terminus a quo*, the irreducible basis for any approach to ecumenical reunion of churches. Although this has been restated in varying formulations by different Lambeth Conferences and different General Conventions over the subsequent decades,[1] yet as recently as 1982 the General Convention of the Episcopal Church specified that the Historic Episcopate of the Chicago-Lambeth Quadrilateral is "central to this apostolic ministry and essential to the reunion of the church."[2] The Anglican participants in the Anglican-Lutheran International Conversation (ALIC) stated in the Pullach Report of 1972 that they could not "foresee full integration of ministries (full communion) apart from the historic episcopate."[3] In LED II, this commitment to the historic episcopate was reaffirmed by Anglicans "as essential in any organic reunion or full communion;"[4] and they added that "acceptance of the historic episcopate remains a pre-condition for full communion and/or organic reunion."[5]

8.   Lutherans, on the other hand, have opposed the notion that the historic episcopate is required as a *condition* for full communion. At Pullach the Lutherans stated that "since the particular form of

episcope is not a confessional question for Lutherans, the historic episcopate should not become a necessary condition for interchurch relations or church union."[6] In a 1984 report on the historic episcopate, the Lutheran churches in the Lutheran Council in the U.S.A. reaffirmed the traditional Lutheran position "that the historic succession of bishops is not essential for the office of the ministry."[7] In a paper presented during LED I on "Lutheran Conditions for Communion in Holy Things," Professor Robert W. Jenson summarized the Lutheran conviction that for the true unity of the church it is enough to proclaim the gospel according to a pure understanding of it and to administer the sacraments according to the Word of God. "If other parties can affirm" this about Lutherans,

> they have no right to demand further uniformities as conditions of communion. Indeed, Lutherans have generally regarded any tendency by another party to make further demands for uniformity as *prima facie* evidence that the gospel is not being preached rightly in that quarter. Here is the place where negotiations between Anglicans and Lutherans have repeatedly broken down around the world. The sticking point has been, of course, the episcopacy.[8]

9.   The historic impasse, as we have inherited it, seems simple but irreconcilable. If Anglicans insist on the historic episcopate as an essential dimension of the church's catholicity and therefore as a precondition for full communion, then Lutherans insist that something is being added to the gospel; and therefore the gospel itself is being undermined if not actually vitiated. For, according to Lutherans,

> The true unity of the church, which is the unity of the body of Christ and participation in the unity of the Father, Son, and Holy Spirit, is given in and through proclamation of the gospel in Word and sacrament. This unity is expressed as a communion in the common and at the same time, multiform confession of one and the same apostolic faith. It is a communion in holy baptism and in the eucharistic meal, a communion in which the ministries exercised are recognized by all as expressions of the ministry instituted by Christ in his church. It is a communion where diversities contribute to fullness and are no longer barriers to unity. It is a committed fellowship, able to make common decisions and to act in common.[9]

Anglicans are convinced that catholicity is being compromised. Lutherans are convinced that "evangelicity" (the gospel) is being compromised. At the 1987 Niagara Falls Anglican-Lutheran Consul-

20

tation on "Episcope in Relation to the Mission of the Church Today," from which *The Niagara Report* eventually emerged, Professor Stephen Sykes, then Canon of Ely Cathedral and Regius Professor of Divinity at Cambridge University, prefaced his response to a paper on "Episcope in the New Testament" with "a deeply felt personal word."

> The frustrating character of the historic disagreement between Anglicans and Lutherans — its sheer folly — can be formulated thus. Anglicans say to Lutherans, "If you have no objection in principle to episcopal government, then your refusal to adopt it can only be obstinacy." Lutherans say to Anglicans, "Of course we can adopt it, provided you Anglicans say it is not necessary for us to do so." To which Anglicans reply, "We haven't got any official theology which says that it, the episcopate, is of the essence of the Church, but we couldn't possibly say, dogmatically, that it wasn't." This conversation is not merely frustrating, it is dumb. And our parent bodies ought to demand their money back from us if in this consultation we cannot show a way out of this ludicrous impasse. It is my conviction that all the necessary elements of deliverance have been placed by God in our hands. God wants us to work at it and to think and pray our way to a solution."[10]

This comment not only states the impasse sharply. It also expresses the conviction that the impasse can be overcome.

10. The impasse is more complex than the foregoing summary would indicate; but happily, in the analysis of its constituent elements, a resolution has begun to emerge as the result of more recent theological developments shared in both churches. Another way of stating the historic impasse on the topic of ordained ministry that has divided Anglicans and Lutherans in the past is by the questions of Professor J. Robert Wright, in a paper that was earlier circulated to the members of LED III:

> 1) Is it possible to possess the substance (*res*) of apostolicity without the sign (*signum*) of episcopal succession? Lutherans would say, certainly yes; Anglicans would be less certain, not unanimous, but would tend to say no.
> 2) Is it possible to possess the sign (*signum*) of episcopal succession without the substance (*res*) of apostolicity? Lutherans would say, certainly, yes; Anglicans again would be less certain but would tend to say no.

Wright rejected this impasse, however, as no longer helpful, remarking,

Do not these questions also pose the issue too sharply, demanding
answers that are more harsh than helpful, and is it not possible to find
a way forward that does not necessitate judgments upon the past and
the present?[11]

11. One major catalyst, cited by Wright, that has helped the churches
to understand and move beyond the impasse on this point was the
1982 Lima Statement on Baptism, Eucharist, and Ministry from the
Faith and Order Commission of the World Council of Churches,
which (in paragraph 38 of its Ministry section) described the episcopal succession "as a sign, though not a guarantee, of the continuity
and unity of the Church." The Lima Statement went on (in paragraph
53) to propose, for implementation of this principle in the cause of
unity, that "Churches which have preserved the episcopal succession
are asked to recognize both the apostolic content of the ordained
ministry which exists in churches which have not maintained such
succession and also the existence in these churches of a ministry of
episkope in various forms." The 1985 General Convention of the
Episcopal Church endorsed this paragraph from Lima as a way
forward for its representatives to pursue in the ecumenical discussions of LED III.[12]

12. From the Lutheran side, clear acknowledgement that this ap-
proach sets the impasse in a new perspective and meets traditional
Lutheran concerns has been forthcoming from the pen of Professor
George Lindbeck:

> What the Reformers objected to was the idea that succession consti-
> tutes a guarantee or criterion of apostolic faithfulness, but once one
> thinks in terms of the sign value of continuity in office, this difficulty
> vanishes. Signs or symbols express and strengthen the reality they
> signify, but the sign can be present without the reality, and the reality
> without the sign (as, for example, is illustrated by the relation of the
> flag and patriotism). Thus it is apostolicity in faith and life that makes
> the episcopal sign fruitful, not the other way around, but this ought
> not be turned into an excuse for neglecting the sign.[13]

If the sign/substance way of understanding the impasse has been
resolved by a deeper perception of the category of "sign" such as
Lima developed, then this really constitutes (in Lindbeck's words) "a
shift in the perception of the diachronic dimension, that is, in the way
in which succession and apostolicity are perceived."

13. Still another element of the impasse, functional *versus* ontological, has also been transcended by developments in historical and theological perception that are shared in both churches. The historic episcopal succession has traditionally been seen by "high church" Anglicans as being ontological, even an essential element of the gospel given for all time, whereas "low church" Lutherans have traditionally emphasized that the ordained ministry is strictly functional in character, having no ontological dimension whatsoever, especially insofar as ordination might then be seen as establishing a superior or higher class of Christians within the church. But now, increasingly within both churches, ordination — and even the office of bishop — is being seen by historians, theologians, and others as being functional in origin and ontological upon reflection. Once the historically functional origin is agreed, there can then also be agreement, as is obvious, that the reflection upon ordained ministry — even by the laity of both churches — does indeed posit a certain "ontological" dimension to it, provided always that it is not accorded a status higher than those whom it serves. Thus Lutheran clergy after ordination, just like clergy of the Episcopal Church, are commonly accorded the title of "The Reverend" in front of their names, indicating some change, but not elevation, of status. Thus it has recently been possible for the Lutheran-United Methodist Dialogue to conclude, on the basis of history, that "a ministry of oversight like that of bishops is a practical necessity."[14] The word "practical" is, of course, a recognition of the functional origin, but the word "necessity," even used in this way, cannot help but posit a certain ontological dimension to the office. It has become possible, therefore, as Lindbeck observes, in view of this shift in perception to use "a functional view of ministry in support of episcopacy (thus reversing the nineteenth century situation when functional arguments were employed almost exclusively by those opposed to episcopacy)."[15]

14. In all these ways, then, the historic impasse has proven to be more complex than had been thought, but in the analysis of its constituent elements a resolution has begun to emerge that now points a way forward.

2

Theological Consensus

15. A basis for convergence has been in the process of formation for a number of decades. Many of the factors which make up this basis are the direct consequence of the nearly one hundred years of Lutheran-Anglican dialogue which have taken place in Europe, the U.S.A., and elsewhere. Special progress has been made in the U.S.A. dialogues since 1968. Historical and theological factors, some more recently recognized, have also contributed to the convergence of the Lutheran and Anglican traditions. The following chapters of the Report seek to identify these factors, often in considerable detail, because it is necessary to provide as much documentation as possible in order to ground adequately the recommendations of the Concordat of Agreement.

THE CONTRIBUTION OF THE MORE RECENT DIALOGUES IN THE U.S.A. AND ABROAD

A. Theological Consensus on the Gospel

16. From its beginnings the church recognized that consensus in the confession of the apostolic gospel was essential to the communion, the unity, of the church. In one of the earliest documents of the Christian movement, the letter to the Galatians, Paul writes:

> I am astonished that you are so quickly deserting him who called you in the grace of Christ and turning to a different gospel — not that there is another gospel, but there are some who trouble you and want to pervert the gospel of Christ. But even if we, or an angel from heaven,

24

should preach to you a gospel contrary to that which we preached to you, let him be accursed. As we have said before, so now I say again, If any one is preaching to you a gospel contrary to that which you received, let him be accursed. (Gal. 1:6-9)

The very existence of a *canon* of the New Testament, with its exclusions as well as its inclusions, testifies to the church's need for and commitment to a standard for orthodoxy in distinction from and in rejection of heresy. The inclusion of four different Gospels in the canon of the New Testament, as well as the inclusion of occasional writings by various authors, testifies to the fact that consensus on the gospel does not require uniformity of expression. However, "the ancient church was never in doubt that unity in doctrine belonged to the conditions for eucharistic communion, and that no teacher of false doctrine might commune with an orthodox congregation."[1]

17.   As a matter of historical record, the Lutheran churches and the Anglican churches have not engaged in doctrinal controversy with each other on the nature of the gospel, nor do their doctrinal documents contain any official condemnation of each other's doctrine. The Lutheran-Episcopal Dialogues in the U.S.A. have confirmed that there is, indeed, consensus on the gospel between our churches. The initial dialogue report (LED I) included summary statements on Holy Scripture, Christian Worship, Baptism-Confirmation and Apostolicity.[2] The second dialogue report (LED II) included joint statements on justification, on the gospel, on eucharistic presence, on the authority of Scripture, and on apostolicity.[3] The current dialogue (LED III) has already published a comprehensive theological statement, *Implications of the Gospel*, in which the eschatological perspective of the New Testament is used to give expression to our agreement on the gospel and its implications for the church's dogma, ecclesiology, and mission. The church as witness to the Reign of God in its worship, doctrine, and polity is identified as the primary implication of the gospel. The church's mission in the midst of the life of the world is addressed in terms of ecumenism, evangelization, and ethics.

18.   A similar consensus was expressed in the reports of the European and international conversations between Lutherans and Anglicans. The consensus was summarized in *The Niagara Report* (1987), paragraphs 61-70:

61 We accept the authority of the canonical Scriptures of the Old and New Testaments. We read the Scriptures liturgically in the course of the Church's year (LED II, 1980, pp. 30-1; *Pullach Report*, 17-22).

62 We accept the Niceno-Constantinopolitan and Apostles' Creeds and confess the basic Trinitarian and Christological Dogmas to which these creeds testify. That is, we believe that Jesus of Nazareth is true God and true Man, and that God is authentically identified as Father, Son and Holy Spirit (LED II, p. 38; *Pullach Report*, 23-25).

63 Anglicans and Lutherans use very similar orders of service for the Eucharist, for the Prayer Offices, for the administration of Baptism, for the rites of Marriage, Burial, and Confession and Absolution. We acknowledge in the liturgy both a celebration of salvation through Christ and a significant factor in forming the *consensus fidelium*. We have many hymns, canticles, and collects in common *(Helsinki Report*, 29-31).

64 We believe that baptism with water in the name of the Triune God unites the one baptized with the death and resurrection of Jesus Christ, initiates into the One, Holy, Catholic and Apostolic Church, and confers the gracious gift of new life *(Helsinki Report*, 22-25).

65 We believe that the Body and Blood of Christ are truly present, distributed and received under the forms of bread and wine in the Lord's Supper. We also believe that the grace of divine forgiveness offered in the sacrament is received with the thankful offering of ourselves for God's service (LED II, pp. 25-29; *Helsinki Report*, 26-28).

66 We believe and proclaim the gospel, that in Jesus Christ God loves and redeems the world. We 'share a common understanding of God's justifying grace, i.e. that we are accounted righteous and are made righteous before God only by grace through faith because of the merits of our Lord and Saviour Jesus Christ, and not on account of our works or merit. Both our traditions affirm that justification leads and must lead to "good works"; authentic faith issues in love' *(Helsinki Report*, 20; cf. LED II, pp. 22-23).

67 Anglicans and Lutherans believe that the Church is not the creation of individual believers, but that it is constituted and sustained by the Triune God through God's saving action in word and sacraments. We believe that the Church is sent into the world as sign, instrument and foretaste of the kingdom of God. But we also recognize that the Church stands in constant need of reform and renewal *(Helsinki Report*, 44-51).

68 We believe that all members of the Church are called to participate in its apostolic mission. They are therefore given various
ministries by the Holy Spirit. Within the community of the Church
the ordained ministry exists to serve the ministry of the whole people
of God. We hold the ordained ministry of word and sacrament to be
a gift of God to his Church and therefore an office of divine institution
(*Helsinki Report*, 32-42).

69 We believe that a ministry of pastoral oversight (*episcope*), exercised in personal, collegial and communal ways, is necessary to
witness to and safeguard the unity and apostolicity of the Church
(*Pullach Report*, 79).

70 We share a common hope in the final consummation of the
kingdom of God and believe that we are compelled to work for the
establishment of justice and peace. The obligations of the Kingdom
are to govern our life in the Church and our concern for the world.
'The Christian faith is that God has made peace through Jesus "by the
blood of his Cross" (Col. 1:20) so establishing the one valid center for
the unity of the whole human family' (Anglican-Reformed International Commission 1984: *God's Reign and Our Unity*, 18 and 43; cf.
Pullach Report, 59).[4]

B. Emerging Convergence of the Dialogues on the Meaning of Apostolicity, Apostolic Succession, and Historic Episcopate

19. Already in the first dialogue (LED I) representatives of our
churches were able to arrive at "five substantive agreements" about
apostolicity.

1. We agree that apostolicity belongs to the reality of the one holy
catholic church; apostolicity is manifested in various ways in all areas
of the church's life, and is guarded especially by common confession
and through that function of the church designated as *episcope*
(oversight).

2. We agree that both our communions can and should affirm that the
Eucharistic celebrations held under the discipline of either communion are true occurrences of the Body of Christ in the world. We agree
that both our communions can and should affirm that the ordained
ministries of both communions are true ministries of the one church
of Christ, that is, that they are apostolic ministries. We agree that
mutual recognition of ministries by each of the two traditions could

27

create the conditions by which both communions could enter that sort of relationship in which each would receive gifts from the other for greater service to the Lord and his Gospel.

3. We agree that the identity of our gospel with the apostles' Gospel, and of our church with the apostles' church, is the personal identity of the risen Christ; He is always the one crucified under Pontius Pilate and just so the one whose word is new promise in every new historical occasion. The church is able to remain in conversation with this one Lord, and so to remain itself through the opportunities and temptations of its history, by the mediation of the whole continuous tradition of the Gospel in word and sacrament. The church has, within the providence of God, enacted its responsibility that this succession shall be a succession of the *Gospel*, by the means of a canon of Scripture, the use and authority of creeds and confessions, sacramental-liturgical tradition, and the institution of an ordered ministry and succession of ministers.

4. We agree that this substance of apostolic succession must take different forms in differing places and times, if the Gospel is indeed to be heard and received. At the time of the Reformation, one of our communions in its place experienced the continuity of the episcopally ordered ministry as an important means of the succession of the Gospel; in various ways the other in its place was able to take its responsibility of the succession of the Gospel only by a new ordering of its ministry. We agree that by each decision the apostolicity of the ministry in question was preserved, and that each of our communions can and should affirm the decision of the other. Until the Lord of the church grants a new ordering of the church, each communion should respect the right of the other to honor the distinct history which mediates its apostolicity, and to continue that ordering of its ministry which its history has made possible. Within the one church, both the Anglican continuity of the episcopal order, and the Lutheran concentration on doctrine, have been means of preserving the apostolicity of the one church.

5. For the future, we agree that if either communion should be able to receive the gift of the other's particular apostolicity, without unfaithfulness to its own, the future of the church would surely be served. In any future ordering of the one church, there will be a ministry and within that ministry an *episcope*. The functional reality of *episcope* is in flux in both our communions. If we are faithful, we will *together* discover the forms demanded by the church's new opportunities, so that the church may have an *episcope* which will be an *episcope* of the apostolic Gospel. Similarly, any future unity of the church will be a unity of common confession. The functional reality

28

of the common confessions of the past (their contemporary interpretation and use) is in flux in both our communions. Our faithfulness will be that we think and pray together seeking to be ready for a new common confession when the Lord shall give us the apostolic boldness to proclaim the Gospel with the freshness and vigor of our fathers in the faith.[5]

No doubt influenced in part by this agreement reached in the LED I dialogue, and citing previous work done in the Faith and Order Commission of the World Council of Churches, the Episcopal Church's Joint Commission on Ecumenical Relations soon adopted a "working statement" on the same subject which it reported to that Church's 1976 General Convention, subtitled "The Relation of the Historic Episcopate to Apostolic Succession," which took the following position:

> The Episcopal Church, through its membership in the Anglican Communion has received and preserved the historic episcopal succession as an effective sign of the continuity of the Church in apostolic faith and mission — manifested in community, doctrine, proclamation, sacraments, liturgy and service.
>
> Any plan for the reunion of the Church should, we insist, preserve a succession in the ordained ministry which assures the fullness of *episcope* as a Gift of God.
>
> We acknowledge, however, that apostolicity has many strands. We see a genuine apostolicity in those churches which, while preserving a continuity in apostolic faith, mission and ministry, have not retained the historic episcopate.
>
> This acknowledgment is based in part on our appreciation that many episcopal functions may be preserved in a church which does not use the title "bishop," provided ordination is always done in it by persons in whom such a church recognizes the authority to transmit ministerial commission.
>
> We believe the importance of the historic episcopate is not diminished by our close association with such a church. On the contrary, insights gained from such associations often enable churches without the historic episcopate to appreciate it as a sign of, and element in, the continuity and unity of the Church.
>
> We rejoice that more and more non-episcopal churches, including those with whom we are having unity consultations, are expressing a willingness to see the historic episcopate as a sign and means of the apostolic succession of the whole Church in faith, life and doctrine, and that it is, as such, something that ought to be striven for when absent.

We affirm the desire of our Church to seek ways to promote continuing and growing fellowship with such churches in our pilgrimage together toward full unity.

The Joint Commission on Ecumenical Relations invited study and response on these two statements, the paragraphs from the World Council Study and the one drafted by JCER itself, looking toward the time when they, or some variation on them, might be

an acceptable stance for the Episcopal Church to take in unity consultations when we are asked to define the meaning of the fourth provision in the Chicago-Lambeth Quadrilateral.[6]

20.   The second dialogue between Lutherans and Episcopalians (LED II) built on the five earlier agreements of LED I. Its achievement was to make explicit the distinction between apostolic succession and the institution of the historic episcopate. It will be sufficient for our purposes to summarize the lengthy "Joint Statement on Apostolicity" with its appendices.[7] In Part One, "Apostolicity: A New Appreciation," apostolicity is defined as "the Church's continuity with Christ and the apostles in its movement through history." Apostolic succession is "a dynamic, diverse reality" embracing faithfulness to apostolic teaching; participation in baptism, prayer, and the eucharist; "sharing in the Church's common life of mutual edification and caring, served by an ecclesiastically called and recognized pastoral ministry of Word and sacrament;" and "continuing involvement in the apostolic mission" of the church by proclaiming the gospel through word and deed. Apostolic succession is not to be understood "primarily in terms of historic episcopate."

21.   Part Two is devoted to a historical description of "Lutheran and Episcopalian Views and Expressions of Apostolic Succession." Part Three contains "An Analysis of the Agreement in Apostolic Succession to be Found in the Lutheran and Episcopal Churches." Both churches agree that apostolic mission means the obedience to the call of Christ to "go into all the world" with the gospel, although the actual obedience of both churches has varied, and both "have had glorious moments and sad declines in this aspect of apostolic succession." Both churches agree in acknowledging the normative character of the apostolic Scriptures and the catholic creeds. Both churches agree that apostolic succession includes obedience to Christ's commands to baptize, to forgive sins, and to share in the eucharist.

22. The ordained ministry is recognized as the "most controversial area" between Lutherans and Episcopalians. But even here there is "a great measure of agreement not always found with other communions." There is agreement that the ordained ministry of Word and Sacrament is "of divine institution," that ordination is an unrepeated liturgical act presided over "by those set apart in the Church so to ordain in the Name of God," that succession of ordained ministers in office shows the church's continuity in time and space, and that there is a necessary oversight (*episkope*) "which is embodied in an ordained office." Finally,

> Episcopalians recognize that Lutherans do affirm the full dignity of the pastoral office and are open to the historic episcopate as a valid and proper form of that office. Some Lutheran Churches are ordered in the historic episcopate. There is even a preference for the historic episcopate shown in the Lutheran confessional writings where and when that form could be maintained in accord with the Gospel, i.e., in the context of faithful preaching of the Word and the right administration of the Sacraments. Lutherans do not, however, hold the historic episcopate to be the only legitimate form of *episcope*.[8]

23. In making the distinction between "apostolic succession" and "historic episcopate" LED II anticipated the formulations of the Lima Statement on Ministry, Section IV, which deals with "Succession in the Apostolic Tradition." In the Lima document "apostolic tradition" is defined as

> continuity in the permanent characteristics of the Church of the apostles: witness to the apostolic faith, proclamation and fresh interpretation of the Gospel, celebration of baptism and the eucharist, the transmission of ministerial responsibilities, communion in prayer, love, joy and suffering, service to the sick and the needy, unity among the local churches and sharing the gifts which the Lord has given to each. (BEM, Ministry, Par. 34)

"Apostolic succession" or "apostolicity" is then understood in terms of Christ's *mission*, and it is defined as "an expression of the permanence and, therefore, of the continuity of Christ's own mission in which the Church participates." (Par. 35)

24. These insights were given further expression in *The Niagara Report*. The life of the early church as it comes to expression in the documents of the New Testament indicates that succession in ministerial

31

office cannot be regarded "as the sole criterion of faithfulness to the apostolic commission." (*The Niagara Report*, Par. 20) The church's "apostolicity" here refers to the church's "mission."

> For apostolicity means that the Church is sent by Jesus to *be* for the world, to participate in his mission and therefore in the mission of the One who sent Jesus, to participate in the mission of the Father and the Son through the dynamic of the Holy Spirit. (Par. 21)

Continuity and succession are, therefore, testimony to *God's* faithfulness in the midst of the church's sin, ambiguity, and unfaithfulness (Paras. 28-30), an accent by which *The Niagara Report* "avoids the triumphalism that too often accompanies . . . descriptions of the church in ecumenical documents."[9]

C. Mutual Understanding of Unity

25.   LED II already demonstrated the broad areas of agreement between Lutherans and Episcopalians on the doctrine of ministry. Attention to a growing consensus on the doctrine of ministry continued in LED III. This can perhaps be best illustrated by summarizing several papers which were presented early in the dialogue (sessions 2 and 3) and to which the dialogue returned later (session 11). In June, 1984, Professor L. William Countryman (Episcopalian) presented a paper on "The Gospel and the Institutions of the Church With Particular Reference to the Historic Episcopate."[10]   In this paper Countryman pointed out that the *goal* of salvation is, in the language of John 17, "the communion of perfect love within God and among God and humanity." In the New Testament writings generally, the gift and goal is not only to be fully realized in the *eschaton*. Unity is the calling and objective of the Christian community here and now. The early Christians' recognition of this goal was the driving force behind a centuries-long process of shaping institutions which could sustain unity in the community. These institutions had their roots in the New Testament era, but they achieved classical form — the form they retained for centuries thereafter — only in the second to tenth centuries. Four such institutions arose: 1) the ritual complex centered on the sacraments of baptism and the eucharist (in classical form by the mid-second century); 2) the threefold ministry (widespread by the late second century); 3) summary statements of Christian belief (taking on familiar form in the late second and the third centuries); and 4) the New Testament canon (largely solidified in the

third and fourth centuries). Each of these "institutions" had a particular *use* in the service of the gospel, and each of them was also subject to abuse. "No one institution, however venerable, can be understood to be of the *esse* of the church; only the gospel is that."[11] The church can be and function without any or all of these institutions, including the threefold ministry. But by looking at the actual ordination rites of *The Apostolic Tradition* of Hippolytus, the earliest such rites in the church's history (ca. 210 c.e.), Countryman observed that the symbolic function of the various ordinations, and therefore of the ministries of bishop, presbyter, and deacon, is "to point to the ministerial nature of the whole body, to its articulation of its own life in the present and to its continuity with Christ through the long chain of people who have heard and then proclaimed the Gospel." Countryman said that in the context of the continental Reformation, it was necessary to break the episcopal succession for the sake of the gospel. He further said, and LED III agrees, that it is not necessary to call that decision into question. "Let it be taken for granted that it was the right course at those places and times."[12] Instead, in his view, the succession was transferred to presbyters, so that now we have two different kinds of succession in the two churches, Anglican and Lutheran, neither of which accomplishes the same symbolic purpose, but neither of them *antithetical* to the other. Countryman's conclusion:

> The historic episcopate contains an element of the proclamation of the Gospel not contained in the Reformation successions — *and vice versa*. The historic episcopate declares to us that the Gospel is not only an idea or a proposition or a proclamation, but the animating force of a living community communicated over and over again from one person to another. The bishop, in this succession, is thus a living image of the unity of the faithful in and with God, a unity yet to be consummated but already at work in us across the barriers of time and space. The Reformation successions also have a message for us: that the Gospel is always transcendent and never merely identical with any of the institutions to which it has given rise among us; if the institutions fail, that does not mean that the gospel has failed nor that the church has ceased. God is perfectly free to make new beginnings with the people.[13]

The two successions are neither identical nor antithetical. Since we believe that the Spirit has given utterance to both, the challenge is "to find ways of sharing and preserving both messages."[14]

26.   In his response, Professor Paul Berge (Lutheran) expressed the importance for the dialogue to come to an understanding of God's gift of ministry to the Christian church:

> The biblical traditions do not present one understanding of how ministry is to be carried out. Therefore, it is incumbent upon us to recognize this and to realize that not one position on ministry is right — or even more righteous — than the other. The interrelationship of the tradition centering on the Word of God and the tradition of a more highly developed ecclesiastical structure for that Word, has been with us since the beginnings of the fledgling Christian communities in the first and second centuries. Likewise, our common heritage from the 16th century is too intertwined and important to the church catholic to even pose the possibility that something is missing in either tradition.[15]

In identifying the concern of LED III for both churches, Berge goes on to say:

> Lutheran-Episcopal Dialogues I and II have left for us the task of coming to an understanding on the issue of ministry. But can it be settled by asking the questions, what do you want of us, or what do we want of you? If "adoption" into historic episcopal succession is what you will require of Lutherans on the basis of the Fourth Quadrilateral, then, this will divide us, not unify us. It can be no other, given our tradition. If Anglicans perceive that we are not convinced that they are clear about the gospel, then what does this mean for your church and ministry? The truth of the gospel and its ministry is that the church is not ours to negotiate, but we are one in God's mission in the world—*missio Dei.*[16]

Drawing upon a theology of the Word of God in the Old Testament and Johannine traditions, Berge concluded that "the tradition of the Fourth Gospel and the tradition of Lutheranism are centered in the living voice of the Word of God."[17] On this issue Countryman and Berge are in fundamental agreement. The ministry can neither take precedence nor preside over the gospel. Berge says, "the lesson Lutherans and Anglicans have learned from history is that when the ecclesiastical system is unwilling to reform, the only word capable of conveying the call for reform is the external truth of the gospel — the Word of God."[18] Hence there can be no creation of an artificial reconciliation of ministries through negotiation. Because we are one in the truth of the gospel we cannot require something of each other which is not essential for salvation. The center for both Lutherans and Episcopalians "is the gospel and its ministry."[19] Countryman would agree, as a later discussion revealed.

27. The dialogue took up both papers again after five years, at Session 11 in June, 1989. Countryman added some "further reflections" which deal even more pointedly with Lutheran concerns as expressed earlier by Berge. He said that we cannot "substitute the ministry of either group for that of the other." But since "our ministries are one way of telling the world who we are," it is necessary for us to think of how our ministries might evolve into something which, in the end, might be "recognizably common." We must re-understand the entire process of ordination, beginning with candidacy and issuing in the actual functioning of ministry, "as a kind of gestural language in which our communities announce, for themselves and each other, who they understand themselves, by God's grace, to be." Ordination can no more be defined simply by the mechanical act of laying on of hands than the eucharist can be defined simply by the mechanical act of reciting the words of institution over the bread and cup. Ordination involves the call and consent of the people of God because it has as much to do with their ministry as with that of the ordinand. Hence the symbolic gestures. Countryman summarizes:

> To ordain a bishop, three other bishops must lay on hands. Since these will have had to come from neighboring cities, they were, in effect, bringing the new bishop into a larger network and reaffirming the local community's communion with the larger church. The Bishop alone laid hands on deacons to indicate that deacons functioned as extensions of the bishop in serving the church. The intimate connection between the two reemphasized the intimate connection between leadership and servanthood that comes down to us as part of Jesus' teaching. On the other hand, from our earliest records onward, other presbyters share in the laying on of hands when a presbyter is ordained, for the college of presbyters has its own integrity in the local church. While it must function in relation to the larger church, as represented by the bishop, this college also served as the council of elders whose advice could guide and restrain the bishop on behalf of the local community — in effect, an enlarged voice for that community in the deliberations of its leaders.[20]

All of this can become idolatrous, but *abusus non tollit usum*. The point of the symbolic actions was to proclaim that the Christian community receives its identity from the gospel. We can, of course, become so concerned with abuses that we invoke the kind of "purity" concerns which Jesus and his disciples rejected as criteria for the new community of the messianic age (Mark 7:1-13; Rom. 14:14). Countryman applied his insights to both traditions. Episcopalians need to understand that they do not lose the historic episcopate by acknowledging the existing ministry of the ELCA as a true, gospel ministry. Lutherans need to understand that they can revise their ordination rites *for the future* without any hint that the integrity of their present ministries is being challenged or that their continuity with their Reformation heritage is being broken.[21]

D. CONTINUITY AND ADAPTATION OF BASIC ECCLESIAL INSTITUTIONS

28.   The basic institutions, canon of Holy Scripture, creed, sacraments, and ministry, which have long defined the life of the church, have their roots in the New Testament. Yet in their classic forms they are clearly the result of development and adaptation beyond their biblical roots. Our churches have neither repudiated that development nor avoided the necessity for adaptation in the light of the gospel. Our churches share a respect for tradition which is not slavery to the past and an openness to judicious development which is not addiction to novelty.

29. *The canon of scripture* is both oldest and youngest of the four institutions. It is oldest, in that Israel was already developing a canon, which emerging Christianity adopted piecemeal. Most early Christians seem to have preferred the scriptures of Israel in their Greek dress rather than the Hebrew-Aramaic version we now treat as standard; and there were differences as to where the precise boundaries of the canon lay. Still, canon was a given for the early Christians. By the time when 2 Peter was written (perhaps mid-second century), Christians were beginning to develop a canon of their own around writings of Paul (2 Pet. 3:15-16). The canon of four Gospels was broadly (but not universally) accepted among Greek-speaking Christians by the late second century. From the fourth century onward there was growing agreement on the canon of the New Testament, although some debate continued for centuries afterward. To this day the canon of Scripture remains a matter of historical and theological judgment.

30.   While there are no developed *creeds* in the New Testament itself, doctrinal formularies existed from very early times. Paul preserves one, apparently antedating his own ministry, concerned with the meaning of baptism: it declared that baptism abolished social distinctions of ethnicity, sex, and class status (e.g., Gal. 3:27-29). Such formulae as this combined with liturgical expressions of praise (such as "Jesus Christ is Lord") to produce a distinctive, Christian way of speaking about God and Christ. Creedal formulae also arose when intra-Christian conflict made it necessary to defend one theological perspective against another. One example might be the summary of the Pauline theology of grace in Titus 3:4-7. Examples more determinative for the future appeared in the late second century when debates with Gnosticism produced "rules of faith" (Tertullian) or "yardsticks of truth" (Irenaeus)—patterns of instruction (rather than exact verbal prescriptions) designed to rule out any separation between the God of Jesus and the Creator of this world. The basis of the second article of the Apostles' Creed seems to lie in the kerygmatic proclamation evident in the epistles of Paul and the sermons of Acts.[22]   Finally in the late third century we find the beginnings of creeds in the classic sense: precise compositions meant to be memorized word-for-word and recited by catechumens. Such creeds arose from liturgical use in baptism, and were further developed in settling doctrinal controversies at the councils of Nicaea and Constantinople.[23]

31.   The earliest of the church's institutions to reach classic shape were the *sacraments*, baptism and the eucharist. Baptism was the doorway into the Christian community from earliest times. Paul speaks of it often (e.g., I Cor. 1:13-17; Rom. 6:1-11) and Matthew says that the risen Lord commanded its use (Matt. 28:19). We know little about details of practice in the first century; but there may well have been some variation of formula (baptism in the name of Jesus or in that of the Trinity). The narratives of Acts suggest that there was little catechesis preceding it. In the second and third centuries, with the writings of Justin Martyr and Hippolytus, we get a glimpse of more highly developed catechesis and rites. At some point the baptism of infants became more usual than the baptism of adults. Eventually, in the Western Church, confirmation was separated from baptism, a development which is coming under increasing criticism today.[24]

The eucharist reached its classic shape in the second century. The narrative of institution in Paul (1 Cor. 11:23-26) and in the

37

synoptic accounts of the Last Supper shows a eucharist still embedded in the community meal. It is difficult to say exactly when the ceremonies of bread and wine were detached from the meal and made a separate rite; but it happened before the time of Justin Martyr (mid-second century). By then, the sacramental rite had not only been separated from the community meal, but also combined with a kind of synagogue service made up of scripture reading, preaching, and prayer. Accommodations to the era of massive persecution and then to the legalization of Christianity produced the great liturgies of the fourth century, foundations of subsequent Christian worship. We still use them, in revisions made by the reformers and by leaders of the modern liturgical movement.[25]

32. Jesus committed his message to people, not books. Therefore *ministry*, as proclamation of the oral gospel and its truth (I Cor. 1:23-24; Gal. 2:5, 14), was integral to Christianity from the first. This called forth an apostolic (missionary) leadership which could call communities of the faithful into being and hand the message on. The new communities required leaders of their own. Early on, Paul urged respect for and obedience to local leaders who devoted themselves to the service of the community (I Thess. 5:12-13; 1 Cor. 16-15-16; Rom. 16:1-2, Phoebe). He addressed the Philippians as a community with "bishops and deacons" (Phil. 1:1). In late New Testament documents, such as the Pastoral Epistles, we find an ongoing concern for the tradition of gospel teaching (e.g., 1 Tim. 1:3-11, 6:20; 2 Tim. 1:12, 2:2) joined with a relatively newer concern for the regularization of local ministerial succession. These letters envisage several orders of ministry (e.g., presbyters, bishops, deacons, widows; cf. 1 Tim. 3:1-13, 5:3-22; Titus 1:5-9). By the early second century, as the letters of Ignatius show, the threefold ministry of bishop, presbyter, and deacon was establishing itself in the provinces of Syria and Asia. By the late second century, it was also found in Gaul and, beginning at least with Victor (end of the second century), in the relatively conservative church at Rome.[26] In time, this threefold ministry became normative in most of Christendom.[27]

33. Both the New Testament grounding of these fundamental institutions of church life and their openness to subsequent development are important. That these have come to be known in classic forms which have served the church well is hereby gratefully acknowledged. Both Lutherans and Anglicans respect tradition. That these institutions have been subject to abuse and misuse, also, but not only,

by Lutherans and Anglicans, must be confessed. Both Lutherans and Anglicans join other Christians in recognizing the normative doctrinal character of the canon of Scripture. Both Lutherans and Anglicans join other Christians in recognizing the normative doctrinal authority of the Apostles' and Nicene creeds. Both Lutherans and Anglicans insist that the sacraments of baptism and the Lord's Supper be administered "with unfailing use of Christ's words of institution, and of the elements ordained by Him"[28] even though both churches as well as most other Western churches have recently reformed the rites of administration and envision future reform. Finally, both Lutherans and Anglicans recognize that the ordained ministry in its various developed forms, including the historic episcopate, is a gift of God to the church. And both of us agree that the historic episcopate can be "locally adapted in the methods of its administration to the varying needs of the nations and peoples called of God into the Unity of His Church."[29] The two subsequent chapters of this report will indicate, among other things, the way in which our two churches have "locally adapted" the episcopate.

3

The Lutheran Churches and Episcopal Ministry

A. Developments within the History of Lutheran Churches

34. The introduction of the Lutheran reforms in various principalities and free cities of the German empire and in various countries of Northern Europe produced different forms of oversight for the churches, each standing in greater or lesser continuity with the inherited traditions and polities of the medieval church.[1] The situation in Germany proved to be the most radical break with the existing church structure, although the temporal authorities appealed "to late medieval precedents" when they "took over functions that belonged to the bishops."[2] In 1520 Martin Luther rejected the medieval sacramental interpretation of ordination,[3] a position that later was closely reflected in Article XXV of the Thirty Nine Articles of Religion.[4] By 1523 Luther had urged the Bohemians "to forego papal ordinations" because no one should be set over a congregation without the knowledge and election of the people.[5] Beginning in 1525 there were non-episcopal ordinations in several territories.[6] The complex history of developments within Germany included the fact that some dioceses and territories did have bishops from the Lutheran movement for a time: Naumburg, 1542-1547; Schleswig-Holstein, 1542-1551; Merseburg, 1544-1550; and Kammin, 1545-1556.[7] It is helpful to note that all of these bishops were installed before Luther's death, three of them in Saxony (Naumburg, Merseburg, and Kammin), and at least Naumburg with his active participation.[8] By the time of the Religious Peace of Augsburg in 1555, the civil authorities were more or less firmly in charge of the administration of church

affairs in the principalities where the reformation had been introduced.[9] For although the Religious Peace of Augsburg merely *suspended* the authority of the traditional bishops, "the leaders in the Protestant territories viewed this proviso rather quickly as the transferral of the episcopal authority to the territorial princes. . . .(and) the territorial prince was looked upon at the same time as being the bishop of his territorial Church."[10] The civil authorities discharged their episcopal responsibilities through consistories, superintendents, and other institutions which often bore a greater resemblance to civil than to ecclesiastical government.[11]

> Wuerttemberg enacted a "church order" (*Kirchenordnung*) that established a consistory consisting of theologians responsible for the examination of ordinands and political councilors responsible for legal and financial affairs. A superintendent was appointed by the duke. Superintendents were soon divided into three ranks: special superintendents, who had local jurisdiction; four regional superintendents to exercise general supervision; and a "dean" to supervise the other superintendents. This form of episcopacy became the model for many German territorities, although the titles sometimes changed.[12]

The end of the German monarchy in 1918 brought with it the end of church government by the civil authorities. Many of the territorial churches chose to give the title *Landesbischof* to the elected leader of the church. The *Landesbischof* functioned more like an archbishop even when others who shared in the ministry of oversight in a given territorial church did not use or were not given the title of "bishop."[13]

35.   In Denmark, Norway, and Iceland, all ruled by the Danish king at the time of the reformation, the reformation was introduced by Christian III (1503-1559), who had been attracted to the reformation as a result of his studies at Wittenberg, and who became king in 1536 after a two-year civil war. He promptly deposed and imprisoned all the Danish bishops because they had opposed him in the civil war, brought John Bugenhagen, pastor of Wittenberg, to Denmark as his advisor, and had Bugenhagen consecrate seven new bishops on September 2, 1537. There is no evidence at that time that there was much concern about this break in the historic succession. Nor was any attempt made to prevent it.[14] In Sweden there was no conflict between the king and the church on the matter of introducing the reformation. As a result the historic episcopate continued in Sweden,[15] and Sweden was determinative for the restoration of the

historic episcopate in Finland and the Baltic states. None of these countries, however, thought that their relationship with Lutheran churches which did not have the historic episcopate was compromised by the difference.

36. The development of leadership patterns and practices in the Lutheran churches of the United States of America was generally uniform. Until well after the end of the Second World War, all Lutheran churches in the U.S.A. exercised oversight through elected leaders who were given the title "president." In 1970 the American Lutheran Church took the decision to make the title "bishop" an optional use for those leaders who had been serving as presidents of its eighteen regional districts. In 1980 the Lutheran Church in America decided to use the title "bishop" for those leaders who had been serving as presidents of its thirty-three regional synods. When the Association of Evangelical Lutheran Churches came into existence a short time later, it subsequently adopted the title "bishop" for its regional and national leaders. At the time that the title "bishop" was introduced, the intention was that this would mean no change in status, function, or understanding of the office from that which obtained under the title "president."[16] Bishops were elected to specific terms and did not become a separate order of ministry. Nevertheless, it is obvious in all three churches that a development occurred in the office and in the expectations of it as a direct result of the change in title. There was greater regard for the pastoral character of the office and for its function as a symbol of unity. When the Evangelical Lutheran Church in America came into being in 1988 the title of bishop was continued almost without debate.[17] In presiding over and giving leadership to their own synods the synod bishops were given a somewhat enhanced pastoral role, even as their role in the national governing structures of the Evangelical Lutheran Church in America was somewhat reduced in comparison to their role in the former Lutheran Church in America. The constitution of the Evangelical Lutheran Church in America provides for a "Conference of Bishops" with its own staff. The "Conference of Bishops" is recognized as having a "special relationship" with the Evangelical Lutheran Church in America's Division for Ministry and with the Office for Ecumenical Affairs. There are signs that the office of bishop continues to evolve in the Evangelical Lutheran Church in America.

B. The Lutheran Confessional Heritage

37. The interpretation of the Lutheran confessional writings contained in the *Book of Concord* has been the subject of renewed disagreement, especially with regard to the historical meaning of articles of the Augsburg Confession dealing with ministry and episcopacy.[18] The issue is familiar to most of the churches whose history includes the Reformation of the 16th century, namely, whether the Reformation is to be understood as a *corrective* of errors and abuses in the medieval Western church or as *constitutive* of a new and autonomous ecclesial tradition. The argument in favor of a constitutive understanding of the Reformation stresses Luther's opposition to the bishops of Germany, virtually none of whom ultimately came to support the Reformation, as well as the fact that autonomous territorial churches were already coming into being at the time that the Augsburg Confession was being formulated, presented, and defended. The most thorough and exhaustive discussion of the historical circumstances surrounding the Augsburg Confession, including the attitudes and intentions of Martin Luther and Philip Melanchthon, is by Wilhelm Maurer.[19] Because Article XXVIII of the Augsburg Confession is of primary importance in determining what kind of polity the Lutheran reformation permits, it is necessary to summarize briefly the historical circumstances as described by Maurer.

38. Luther's early rejection of the medieval understanding of ordination included a rejection of the necessity for episcopal ordination.[20] Already in 1520 Luther, in his interpretation of one school of medieval theology, thought of bishops and pastors as having virtually interchangeable offices.[21] Writing to the Bohemians in 1523, Luther attacked the ordination of bishops because "they ordain priests to sacrifice rather than to serve the Word, thus perverting the Sacrament." Hence, the right to ordain belongs to the whole church, "especially in cases of emergency when papal bishops refuse to appoint servants of the Word."[22] However, says Maurer, "the emergency situation in Bohemia should not lead one to deduce a general rejection of the historic episcopate." Although there were strong tendencies toward secularization of bishoprics on the part of all parties in Germany, "Luther did not simply condemn the late medieval episcopacy." In 1528 Luther

> retraced the visiting function of the archbishop and bishop, rediscovering traces of it in canonical law, and using the later decline to

show the necessity for this function. He saw the visitations set up by the elector as the beginning of such a restoration. Nevertheless, in no way did he consider this action, and the ecclesiastical offices it created, a substitute for the historic office of bishop.[23]

39. When the emperor summoned the estates to Augsburg in 1530 in order to settle the religious dispute in the empire, the preparations began with proposals for what eventually became Article 28. The proposal presupposed "the continued existence of the medieval hierarchy," and offered a compromise: the reforming territories would recognize again the jurisdiction of the bishops, which had in effect already been lost, if the bishops would not require celibacy and the renunciation of evangelical doctrine by prospective ordinands.[24] Melanchthon won Luther to this compromise by the time the Wittenberg party arrived at Coburg in April of 1530. Luther's commitment to the compromise was the background for his "Exhortation to All Clergy Assembled at Augsburg,"[25] written in May and made available in printed form in Augsburg by early June. "A pact between Lutheran Reformation and the bishops is still possible," wrote Maurer, and that, indeed, was Luther's "top priority" as with "stern love (he) sketches the portrait of a proper Christian bishop."[26]

40. At the heart of Article 28 is "the doctrine of the two ways of governing (two kingdoms)." It is the most fundamental statement on the subject in all of the Lutheran confessional writings. The starting point for the discussion of the spiritual authority of bishops (in contrast to temporal or secular authority) is "the power of the keys, that is, the spiritual authority which is at work in the liturgical events of confession and absolution." The authority of bishops is grounded in the Word of God, that is, the gospel. It is "concentrated in the liturgical events of an ordered church." Rejected as contrary to the proper exercise of episcopal office is all coercion, which is appropriate only to temporal or secular authority.[27]

41. Nothing came of the compromise proposal at Augsburg. The final draft of the *Confutation*, prepared by John Eck and supported by the traditional party, did not refer to the compromise directly. But in the first draft there was summary rejection of everything initiated by the visitations in 1528 of the parishes in Saxony "as in conflict with apostolic ordinances."[28] Meanwhile, in July, Luther continued his apparent attack on the bishops. His blistering *Propositiones adversus totam synagogam Sathanae et universas portas inferorum*[29] contained "the

outlines of ordered church reform that would span all of Christendom." In it Luther defined an appropriate relationship between congregation and bishop which provided for

> the agreement of both parties. . . .The pastor has the right and duty to propose new ordinances and to recommend the amendment or abolition of surviving ones—all of this, however, only with the concurrence of the congregation. . . .It is assumed that all the baptized who believe belong to the congregation. The jurisdiction of the pastor can just as well encompass a province as a city, or even the world; there is room for division into bishoprics, and even for a reformed papacy.[30]

By 1531, Maurer believes, Luther and Melanchthon were once again agreed in support of the compromise proposal. For although Melanchthon was disappointed that the compromise was rejected at Augsburg,

> he stated his continued readiness to retain episcopal authority, the polity of the church. In an opinion issued jointly by Melanchthon and Luther at the end of May 1531, the latter basically approved of his friend's standpoint. From the perspective of suffering obedience, Luther was willing to accept the jurisdiction of bishops, even if they "were wolves and our enemies"—"because they still possess the office and sit in the place of the apostles"—as long as pure doctrine would be guaranteed.[31]

42. On the basis of the historical perspective provided by Wilhelm Maurer it is evident that the Lutheran confessional documents of the 16th century, normative for the Evangelical Lutheran Church in America,[32] endorse the historic episcopate in principle. The Lutheran view, according to these documents, is that an understanding of ministerial offices within the one divinely instituted ministry of Word and Sacraments is important, and these offices are useful to the extent that they serve the ministry of Word and Sacraments.[33] This means that, while Lutherans regard structures of *episkope* as in one sense "adiaphora," they do not consider them unimportant. They are, in fact, no less important than the theological insights of Martin Luther and the documents of the *Book of Concord*, which are also regarded as in one sense "adiaphora."[34] In the Lutheran confessional documents, Lutherans articulated a vision which looks toward a reformed catholic episcopate existing under the gospel and serving the gospel. It is useful to cite at some length the material from the Lutheran confessional writings because the summaries which have

appeared elsewhere[35] do not always convey fully the confessional position.

43.　The princes and cities which presented their confession to Emperor Charles V at the Imperial Diet of Augsburg in 1530 did so in order that the contending parties could resolve the dispute over reform which had been taking place in Germany so that "all of us embrace and adhere to a single, true religion and live together in unity and in one fellowship and church, even as we are all enlisted under one Christ" (Preface to the Augsburg Confession, 4).[36] One cannot simply begin with Article XIV, "Order in the Church," even though in his Apology Melanchthon accepted the interpretation of the phrase "regular call" as *ordinatione canonica* (canonical ordination) on which the opponents had insisted.[37] The "regular call" simply means that "one cannot place oneself in the pastoral office." One is dependent for office on whatever lawful authorities place one into office.[38] It is necessary to begin with Article XXVIII on "The Power of Bishops" which contains the compromise proposal of the evangelical party. At its heart is the attempt to define the authentic spiritual authority of bishops. "Some have improperly confused the power of bishops with the temporal sword" (CA XXVIII,G,1). But "according to the Gospel the power of keys or the power of bishops is a power and command of God to preach the Gospel, to forgive and retain sins, and to administer and distribute the sacraments" (CA XXVIII,G,5).

> This power of keys or of bishops is used and exercised only by teaching and preaching the Word of God and by administering the sacraments (to many persons or to individuals, depending on one's calling). In this way are imparted not bodily but eternal things and gifts, namely, eternal righteousness, the Holy Spirit, and eternal life. These gifts cannot be obtained except through the office of preaching and of administering the holy sacraments, for St. Paul says, "The gospel is the power of God for salvation to everyone who has faith." Inasmuch as the power of the church or of bishops bestows eternal gifts and is used and exercised only through the office of preaching, it does not interfere at all with government or temporal authority. Temporal authority is concerned with matters altogether different from the Gospel (CA XXVIII,G,8-10).

The desire to distinguish political power from the office of bishop was especially necessary in Germany, where many bishops were also secular rulers of the territories included in their dioceses. That this distinction does not imply rejection of episcopacy becomes evident in the conclusion.

> Thus our teachers distinguish the two authorities and the functions of the two powers, directing that *both* be held in honor as the highest gifts of God on earth (CA XXVIII,G,18).

Insofar as the ministry of bishops is a ministry of the gospel they function by "divine right."

> According to divine right,[39] therefore, it is the office of the bishop to preach the Gospel, forgive sins, judge doctrine and condemn doctrine that is contrary to the Gospel, and exclude from the Christian community the ungodly whose wicked conduct is manifest. All this is to be done not by human power but by God's Word alone. On this account parish ministers and churches are bound to be obedient to the bishops according to the sayings of Christ in Luke 10:16, "He who hears you hears me" (CA XXVIII,G,21-22).

However, it is not necessary to obey bishops if they teach or institute anything contrary to the gospel.[40] Article XXVIII now seeks to assign responsibility for the threatening schism to the bishops. The Lutheran reform movement is not seeking to create a new church or institute a new polity.[41] They claim an ancient right to refuse obedience to bishops who teach and issue commands contrary to the gospel.

> St. Augustine also writes in his reply to the letters of Petilian that one should not obey even regularly elected bishops if they err or if they teach or command something contrary to the divine Holy Scriptures. Whatever other power and jurisdiction bishops may have in various matters (for example, in matrimonial cases and in tithes), they have these by virtue of human right (CA XXVIII,G,28-29).

> What are we to say, then, about Sunday and other similar church ordinances and ceremonies? To this our teachers reply that bishops or pastors may make regulations so that everything in the churches is done in good order, but not as a means of obtaining God's grace or making satisfaction for sins, nor in order to bind men's consciences by considering these things necessary services of God and counting it a sin to omit their observance even when this is done without offense. . . .It is proper for the Christian assembly to keep such ordinances for the sake of love and peace, to be obedient to the bishops and parish ministers in such matters, and to observe the

47

regulations in such a way that one does not give offense to another and so that there may be no disorder or unbecoming conduct in the church (CA XXVIII,G,53-55).

The bishops might easily retain the obedience of men if they did not insist on the observance of regulations which cannot be kept without sin. Now, however, they administer the sacrament in one kind and prohibit administration in both kinds. Again, they forbid clergymen (Geistlichen) to marry and admit no one to the ministry unless he first swears an oath that he will not preach this doctrine, although there is no doubt that it is in accord with the holy Gospel. Our churches do not ask that the bishops should restore peace and unity at the expense of their honor and dignity (though it is incumbent on the bishops to do this, too, in case of need), but they ask only that the bishops relax certain unreasonable burdens which did not exist in the church in former times and which were introduced contrary to the custom of the universal Christian church (CA XXVIII,G,69-72).

St. Peter forbids the bishops to exercise lordship as if they had power to coerce the churches according to their will. It is not our intention to find ways of reducing the bishops' power, but we desire and pray that they may not coerce our consciences to sin (CA XXVIII,G,76-77).

The final paragraph was quoted according to the official German text. Here it is important to quote also the official Latin text.

Peter forbids the bishops to be domineering and to coerce the churches. It is not our intention that the bishops give up their power to govern, but we ask for this one thing, that they allow the Gospel to be taught purely and that they relax some few observances which cannot be kept without sin.

The German text concludes:

If they are unwilling to do this and ignore our petition, let them consider how they will answer for it in God's sight, inasmuch as by their obstinacy they offer occasion for division and schism, which they should in truth help to prevent (CA XXVIII,G,78).

44. In his defense of the Augsburg Confession, Philip Melanchthon reiterates the concerns adduced above, and adds this paragraph.

In the Confession we have said what power the Gospel grants to bishops. Those who are now bishops do not perform the duties of bishops according to the Gospel, though they may well be bishops according to canonical polity, *to which we do not object (quam non reprehendimus)*. But we are talking about a bishop according to the Gospel. We like the old division of power into the power of the order and the power of jurisdiction (*potestas ordinis, potestas jurisdictionis*). Therefore a bishop has the power of the order (*Habet igitur episcopus potestatem ordinis*), namely, *the ministry of Word and sacraments*. He also has the power of jurisdiction, namely, the authority to excommunicate those who are guilty of public offenses or to absolve them if they are converted and ask for absolution. A bishop does not have the power of a tyrant to act without a definite law, nor that of a king to act above the law. But he has a definite command, a definite Word of God, which he ought to teach and according to which he ought to exercise his jurisdiction. Therefore it does not follow that since they have a certain jurisdiction bishops may institute new acts of the Word, they have the command about when they should exercise their jurisdiction, namely, when anyone does something contrary to that Word which they have received from Christ.

In the Confession we nevertheless added the extent to which it is legitimate for them to create traditions, namely, that they must not be necessary acts of worship but a means for preserving order in the church, for the sake of peace (Apol. XXVIII,12-15).

Earlier, in his commentary on and defense of Article XIV, on Ecclesiastical Order, Melanchthon both reaffirms the Lutheran commitment to the traditional polity and explains why it has been lost in Germany.

With the proviso that we employ canonical ordination, they accept Article XIV, where we say that no one should be allowed to administer the Word and the sacraments in the church unless he is duly called. *On this matter we have given frequent testimony in the assembly to our deep desire to maintain the church polity and various ranks of the ecclesiastical hierarchy*, although they were created by human authority. We know that the Fathers had good and useful reasons for instituting ecclesiastical discipline in the manner described by the ancient canons. But the bishops either force our priests to forsake and condemn the sort of doctrine we have confessed, or else, in their unheard of cruelty, they kill the unfortunate and innocent men. This keeps our priests from acknowledging such bishops. *Thus the cruelty of the bishops is the reason for the abolition of canonical government (canonica politia) in some places, despite our earnest desire to keep it.* Let them see to it how they will answer to God for disrupting the church.

In this issue our consciences are clear and we dare not approve the cruelty of those who persecute this teaching, for we know that our confession is true, godly, and catholic. We know that the church is present among those who rightly teach the Word of God and rightly administer the sacraments. It is not present among those who seek to destroy the Word of God with their edicts, who even butcher anyone who teaches what is right and true, though the canons themselves are gentler with those who violate them. *Furthermore, we want at this point to declare our willingness to keep the ecclesiastical and canonical polity*, provided that the bishops stop raging against our churches. This willingness will be our defense, both before God and among all nations, present and future, against the charge that we have undermined the authority of the bishops (Apol XIV, 1-5).

The emphasis has been added to point to the fact that churches which accept the doctrinal authority of the *Book of Concord*, as the Evangelical Lutheran Church in America does, are committed in principle to a preference for "the ecclesiastical and canonical polity" with its "various ranks of the ecclesiastical hierarchy."[42] The loss of such "ranks" is here ascribed by Melanchthon to "the cruelty of the bishops," not to outright rejection of bishops, presbyters, and other orders of ministry in the church as a matter of principle or intention.

45. Studies of Martin Luther's understanding of ministry abound,[43] sometimes with emphasis on and interpretations of his antipathy to bishops at certain times in his life. But his views have official standing in the Evangelical Lutheran Church in America only in those writings of his which were taken up into the *Book of Concord*. Luther does not deal with the subject of bishops in either of the catechisms which he prepared in 1529. But in the Smalcald Articles of 1537, prepared in anticipation of an ecumenical council, Luther gives expression to his vision of the ministry of bishops in terms of how he views the church's history and what he would like to see in a reformed church.

Consequently the church cannot be *better* governed and maintained than by having all of us live under one head, Christ, and by having all the bishops equal in office (however they may differ in gifts) and diligently joined together in unity of doctrine, faith, sacraments, prayer, works of love, etc. So St. Jerome writes that the priests of Alexandria governed the churches together and in common. The apostles did the same, and after them all the bishops throughout Christendom, until the pope raised his head over them all (SA, Part II, Article IV, 9).

Later Luther indicates both his willingness to accept the ministry of bishops "for the sake of love and unity" and affirms his conviction, almost from despair, that episcopal ordination is not a necessary feature of church polity.

> If the bishops were true bishops and were concerned about the church and the Gospel, they might be permitted (for the sake of love and unity, but not of necessity, *nicht aus Not*) to ordain and confirm us and our preachers, provided this could be done without pretense, humbug, and unchristian ostentation (*alle Larven und Gespenste unchristliches Wesens und Gepraenges*). However, they neither are nor wish to be true bishops. They are temporal lords and princes who are unwilling to preach or teach or baptize or administer Communion or discharge any office or work in the church. More than that, they expel, persecute, and condemn those who have been called to do these things. Yet the church must not be deprived of ministers on their account.
>
> Accordingly, as we are taught by the examples of the ancient churches and Fathers, we shall and ought ourselves ordain suitable persons to this office. The papists have no right to forbid or prevent us, not even according to their own laws, for their laws state that those who are ordained by heretics shall also be regarded as ordained and remain so. St. Jerome, too, wrote concerning the church in Alexandria that it was originally governed without bishops by priests and preachers in common (SA, Part III, Article X,1-3).

Although Luther here conflates several quotations from St. Jerome, whom he cites from memory, the Roman Catholic participants in the U.S.A. Lutheran-Catholic Dialogue supported Luther's basic conviction:

> 40. When the episcopate and the presbyterate had become a general pattern in the church, the historical picture still presents uncertainties that affect judgment on the Minister of the eucharist. For instance, is the difference between a bishop and a priest of divine ordination? St. Jerome maintained that it was not; and the Council of Trent, wishing to respect Jerome's opinion, did not undertake to define that the preeminence of the bishop over presbyters was by divine law. If the difference is not of divine ordination, the reservation to the bishop of the power of ordaining Ministers of the eucharist would be a church decision. In fact, in the history of the church there are instances of priests (i.e., presbyters) ordaining other priests, and there is evidence that the church accepted and recognized the Ministry of priests so ordained.[44]

46.   The theologians assembled in Smalcald in 1537 did not officially adopt Luther's articles, although they eventually gained official status when they were incorporated into the *Book of Concord*. The theologians did, however, adopt the "Treatise on the Power and Primacy of the Pope" as a confession of faith and intended it as a "supplement to the Augsburg Confession."[45] The fundamental thrust of the treatise is to contest the primacy of the bishop of Rome by divine right, and to contest especially his right to "elect, ordain, confirm, and depose all bishops." During the course of making its case the treatise has much to say about episcopacy. It adduces as "Testimony from History" the following:

> 5.   The Council of Nicaea decided that the bishop of Alexandria should administer the churches in the East and the bishop of Rome should administer the suburban churches, that is, those that were in the Roman provinces in the West . . . (TR, 12).

> 6.   Again, the Council of Nicaea decided that bishops should be elected by their own churches in the presence of one or more neighboring bishops. This was also observed in the West and in the Latin churches, as Cyprian and Augustine testify . . . (TR, 13).

Then the treatise takes up "The Power and Jurisdiction of Bishops."

> In the Confession (Augsburg Confession) and in the Apology we have set forth in general terms what we have to say about ecclesiastical power.

> The Gospel requires of those who preside over the churches that they preach the Gospel, remit sins, administer the sacraments, and, in addition, exercise jurisdiction, that is, excommunicate those who are guilty of notorious crimes and absolve those who repent. By the confession of all, even of our adversaries, it is evident that this power belongs by divine right to all who preside over the churches, whether they are called pastors, presbyters, or bishops. Accordingly Jerome teaches clearly that in the apostolic letters all who preside over the church are both bishops and presbyters. . . .And Jerome observes: "One man was chosen over the rest to prevent schism, lest several persons, by gathering separate followings around themselves, rend the church of Christ. For in Alexandria, from the time of Mark the Evangelist to the time of Bishops Heracles and Dionysius, the presbyters always chose one of their number, set him in a higher place, and called him bishop. Moreover, in the same way in which an army

might select a commander for itself, the deacons may choose from their number one who is known to be active and name him archdeacon. For, apart from ordination, what does a bishop do that a presbyter does not do?" Jerome therefore teaches that the distinction between the grades of bishop and presbyter (or pastor) is by human authority. . . .Afterwards one thing made a distinction between bishops and pastors, and this was ordination, for it was decided that one bishop should ordain the ministers in a number of churches. But since the distinction between bishop and pastor is not by divine right, it is manifest that ordination administered by a pastor in his own church is valid by divine right. Consequently, when the regular bishops become enemies of the Gospel and are unwilling to administer ordination, the churches retain the right to ordain for themselves. For whenever the church exists, the right to administer the Gospel also exists (TR, 60-66).

47. It is clear from these extensive citations that during the "confessional phase" (1528-1537) of the reforming movement, before there were separated evangelical churches no longer under the jurisdiction of Rome,[46] there are consistent statements of commitment to the church's traditional polity, which includes both the historic episcopate and "ranks" in the hierarchy. It is also clear that Lutherans regarded the ministry of bishops to be a ministry of the gospel, that is, a ministry of preaching the Word and administering the Sacraments. This ministry, like that of pastors, is by divine right and institution. In common with the Western catholic tradition, prior to the patristic rediscoveries of the 17th century, they regarded the distinction between bishops and presbyters, and especially the episcopal ministry of ordination, to be of human origin.[47] They did not reject either the distinction or the episcopal ministry of ordination. It is important to stress, however, that the Lutheran reformers believed that one ministerial office as such had been instituted by God: the pastoral office of proclamation of the Word of God and administration of the sacraments. Because they believed that both bishops and presbyters had identical divine authorization, they considered their own ordinations to be valid wherever the canonical bishops refused to ordain clergy for the churches of the reform movement. It must be stressed that for the Lutheran confessional tradition, historical succession of laying-on-of-hands in the ministerial office was not theologically primary. The confessional tradition believes that the divine institution of the ministerial office is evidenced by its faithfulness to and continuity in the apostolic Word and Sacraments as heard and

received in the church throughout the centuries.[48] Thus, Lutherans believe, it is the content, and not the form, of ministry that ultimately authenticates it.[49]

C. THE HISTORIC EPISCOPATE IN LUTHERAN-EPISCOPAL DIALOGUE

48. Lutherans have given unanimous and consistent expression to their confessional heritage on the subject of the historic episcopate in Lutheran-Episcopal Dialogue. At the conclusion of LED I, representatives of each church agreed that the other had preserved "the succession of the Gospel" at the time of the Reformation, although each did so in a different way. This agreement, already cited above in Par. 19, stated:

> One of our communions in its place experienced the continuity of the episcopally ordered ministry as an important means of the succession of the Gospel; in various ways the other in its place was able to take its responsibility for the succession of the Gospel only by a new ordering of its ministry. We agree that by each decision the apostolicity of the ministry in question was preserved, and that each of our communions can and should affirm the decision of the other. . . . Within the one church, both the Anglican continuity of the episcopal order, and the Lutheran concentration on doctrine, have been means of preserving the apostolicity of the one church.[50]

The Lutherans were able to join the Episcopalians in a vision for the future fully consistent with Lutheran openness to the traditional polity and the ministry of the historic episcopate. Together, as cited above in Par. 19, they said:

> For the future, we agree that if either communion should be able to receive the gift of the other's particular apostolicity, without unfaithfulness to its own, the future of the church would surely be served. In any future ordering of the one church, there will be a ministry and within that ministry an *episcope*. The functional reality of *episcope* is in flux in both our communions. If we are faithful, we will *together* discover the forms demanded by the church's new opportunities, so that the church may have an *episcope* which will be an *episcope* of the apostolic Gospel.[51]

As cited earlier, Professor Robert Jenson stated in a concluding essay:

The Lutheran position means that so long as the episcopacy — or any other "ceremony" — is not made an *antecedent condition* of communion, Lutherans are committed to limitless openness thereafter, both in investigating the inadequacy of their own previous arrangements and in achieving new arrangements for future forms of the church. The explicit recognition of "episcope" as an intrinsic function in the church has not been characteristic of Lutheranism; but it in no way violates Lutheran principle, and merely makes up a rather obvious *lacuna* in our thought.[52]

The International Anglican-Lutheran "Pullach Report," as quoted in LED I, states

Since the particular form of episcope is not a confessional question for Lutherans, the historic episcopate should not become a necessary condition for interchurch relations or church union. *On the other hand, those Lutheran churches which have not retained the historic episcopate are free to accept it where it serves the growing unity of the church in obedience to the gospel.*[53]

Gunnar Hultgren, archbishop of Uppsala and Lutheran co-chair of the international dialogue, raised an important question in a personal note attached to the "Pullach Report." While affirming the traditional Lutheran position that "the only necessary condition to full church fellowship is agreement on the truth of the gospel (CA VII)," he asked Lutheran churches whether this necessarily means "that all forms of church order equally serve the church's witness to the truth of the gospel?" In a pointed reformulation, he continued, "Is the absence of the historic episcopate in some Lutheran churches only motivated by faithfulness to the gospel, or have other motives been at work?"[54] Finally, at the end of LED II in 1980, the Lutheran participants in a unanimous "Statement by Lutherans to Lutherans" reached the following conclusion:

Because of what episcopal succession has meant to the church throughout much of its history, and because of its ecumenical significance today, we recommend that the Lutheran Churches in America begin an internal study of the historic episcopate to determine whether it is a viable form of ministry for our Churches. Our report notes that the Lutheran Confessions show a preference for the historic episcopate where and when that ministry can be maintained in the service of the gospel. We are also aware that the Lutheran Churches in Sweden, Finland, and some Lutheran Churches in Africa have bishops in the historic succession. Indeed, the current President of the Lutheran World Federation, Bishop Josiah Kibira of the Northwest Diocese of the Evangelical Lutheran Church in Tanzania, is ordained into the historic episcopate. We are convinced that our willingness to deal seriously with this issue would be regarded as a most positive sign by our Episcopalian brothers and sisters, could serve the cause of church unity, and might redound to our own blessing.[55]

49.   The openness to the "historic episcopate" on the part of Lutherans in the Pullach Report of 1972 has been echoed in subsequent international and other national dialogues with Anglicans. At Helsinki in 1982, the Anglican-Lutheran European Regional Commission (ALERC) reported that in the matter of the "historical succession of bishops"

> there still remains a difference between us because, while Anglicans cannot envisage any form of organic church union without the historic episcopate, Lutheran churches are not able to contribute to the historic episcopate the same significance for organic church union.

At the same time, even though Lutherans

> cannot accept any suggestion that the ministry exercised in their own tradition should be invalid until the moment that it enters into an existing line of episcopal succession. . . .Lutheran theologians and Churches are increasingly prepared to appreciate episcopal succession, in the words of the Faith and Order text (BEM), "as a sign of the apostolicity of the life of the whole Church."[56]

D. Additional Developments

50.   In 1984 the Lutheran member churches of the Lutheran Council in the U.S.A. completed a two-year study of the historic episcopate and published a report. The report can well serve as a summary of the openness of Lutheran churches in the U.S.A. to the possibility of the historic episcopate. The study was occasioned both by the introduction of the title "bishop" for regional leaders elected to the ministry of "oversight" and by the attention being given to the historic episcopate in ecumenical dialogues. After summarizing the results of historical study and the teaching of the Lutheran Confessions, the study concludes as follows:

Some are urging Lutheran churches to adopt the historic episcopate. The "historic episcopate" is variously understood by various churches at the present time, but it usually includes views on the historic succession of bishops. When the "historic episcopate" faithfully proclaims the gospel and administers the sacraments, it may be accepted as a symbol of the church's unity and continuity throughout the centuries provided that it is not viewed as a necessity for the validity of the church's ministry. American Lutheranism is free to create under the guidance of the Spirit forms of leadership that embody *episcope* and hold ecumenical promise.[57]

In a special appendix on the definition of the historic episcopate, the study, repeating for emphasis, concludes:

When the "historic episcopate" faithfully proclaims the gospel and administers the sacraments, it may be accepted as a symbol of the church's unity and continuity throughout the centuries provided that it is not viewed as a necessity for the validity of the church's ministry.[58]

The importance of this conclusion for the task of this dialogue and the future reconciliation of Lutheran and Episcopal ministries ought to be self-evident.

51. The 1982 adoption of *Baptism, Eucharist and Ministry* by the Faith and Order Commission of the World Council of Churches gave encouragement to the developments in Lutheran churches reported above. Despite reservations, there are many features of BEM to which the American Lutheran churches resonated: the "thoroughly theological character of the document, and the seriousness with which it deals with theological issues"; beginning the section on ministry "with an affirmation about the calling and ministry of the whole people of God"; the description of ordained ministry in Paragraph 13; "the description of the authority of the ministry as being derived from the authority of Christ,"[59] the grounding of the ordained ministry in the gospel; the concept of apostolicity; and "the recognition that the advocacy of the Tradition does not require adherence to specific forms of the Tradition."[60] Particularly significant for subsequent developments within the Evangelical Lutheran Church in America is the several-times repeated commendation in *Baptism, Eucharist and Ministry* of the threefold ministry of bishop, presbyter, and deacon as well as commendation of the historic episcopate.[61] For in order to address the issues of ministry left

unresolved at the time of the founding, the constitution of the Evangelical Lutheran Church in America contained the following provision:

> During the . . . period of 1988-1994, this church shall engage in an intensive study of the nature of ministry, leading to decisions regarding appropriate forms of ministry that will enable this church to fulfill its mission. During the course of such study, special attention shall be given to:
> 1) the tradition of the Lutheran church;
> 2) the possibility of articulating a Lutheran understanding and adaptation of the threefold ministerial office of bishop, pastor, and deacon and its ecumenical implication; and
> 3) the appropriate forms of lay ministries to be officially recognized and certified by this church, including criteria for certification, relation to synods, and discipline.[62]

A Task Force on the Study of Ministry, established by the Evangelical Lutheran Church in America in 1988, is now at work under this mandate.

4

The Episcopal Church and the Ministry of the Historic Episcopate

A. The Legacy of the Church of England

52. It is well-known that during the reformations of the 16th century the Church of England maintained the threefold order of the ordained ministry with the episcopate at its heart. Under Henry VIII the royal supremacy replaced papal supremacy and separated England from the jurisdiction of the bishop of Rome. An Act Restraining the Payment of Annates (1534) took for granted the threefold order focused in the episcopate and ordered that from henceforth the king, in his role as Supreme Head of the Church in England, should nominate to the proper electing body the person to be elected archbishop or bishop.[1] In the reign of King Edward VI an ordinal was devised and published in 1550 with the title, "The forme and maner of makynge and consecratyng of Archebishoppes, Bishoppes, Priestes and Deacons." It was revised and bound up with the 1552 Book of Common Prayer and is to be found in subsequent prayer books. The preface to the Ordinal stated "that from the Apostles' time there hath been these orders of Ministers in Christ's Church,"[2] and this was seen as sufficient reason for the continuance of the threefold order.

53. After the brief and troublesome reign of the Roman Catholic Queen Mary, during which doctrinal reforms were reversed and papal jurisdiction reintroduced for a short time, Queen Elizabeth came to the throne, Parliament restored royal supremacy, and the historic episcopate was again set free from the jurisdiction of the bishop of Rome. Elizabeth did not seek the restoration of the Edwardian legislation (repealed under Mary) that had directed the crown to

appoint bishops by letters patent rather than following the traditional canonical procedures. She did clarify the supremacy, claiming rather less than did her father, Henry VIII, preferring to be known as "Governor" rather than "Head" of the church, firmly stating that she did not take to herself any authority other than that provided by law, would not tamper with inherited doctrine or ceremony, and would not claim any "function belonging to any ecclesiastical person being a minister of the Word and Sacraments of the Church."[3] She would, so she signified, maintain the historic order of the Church's ministry and its essential integrity. And yet, although the ancient threefold pattern of the ordained ministry was thus retained under reformation, one significant change from the years of Edward VI may be noted as surviving the tumultuous events of that century: bishops, priests, and deacons were permitted to marry.[4]

54. Anglican attitudes toward the episcopate and understandings of its meaning and functions developed during the 16th and 17th centuries. At the outset there were those who continued to regard bishops as primarily servants of the state. On the other hand there were bishops such as John Hooper who labored diligently in his diocese to provide a learned clergy and to correct the faults of those perceived to be in error, chiefly through the ecclesiastical courts.[5] The expectation of bishops' attendance at court, necessitating long absences from their dioceses, declined markedly under Elizabeth. John Jewel, Queen Elizabeth's first bishop of Salisbury, reflected the Reformation point of view, stating: "Those oily, shaven, portly hypocrites, we have sent back to Rome from whence we first appointed them: for we require our bishops to be pastors, labourers, and watchmen."[6] Although in the early years of Queen Elizabeth's reign there were those who did not take a high view of episcopacy, the dominant attitude of that time was probably expressed by the final Elizabethan archbishop of Canterbury, John Whitgift, who believed that episcopacy best suited monarchical government which, incidentally, he regarded as the best form of government. But where the civil government was oligarchical, he considered, the ecclesiastical government might appropriately be presbyteral,[7] and thus foreigners ordained abroad only by presbyters were allowed to minister in England. But none were to be ordained in England save by bishops. The evidence thus suggests that in the sixteenth and early seventeenth centuries the prevalent theological opinion in the Church of England was that where episcopal ordination was available, it

should be retained; but in cases of necessity where this was not possible, such as on the continent, then presbyteral ordination might suffice. Richard Hooker expressed the Anglican understanding this way:

> When the exigence of necessity doth constrain to leave the usual ways of the church, which otherwise we would willingly keep, where the church must needs have some ordained and neither hath nor can have possibly a bishop to ordain, in case of such necessity, the ordinary institution of God hath given oftentimes, and may give, place. And therefore we are not simply without exception to urge a lineal descent of power from the Apostles by continued succession of bishops in every effectual ordination. These cases of inevitable necessity excepted, none may ordain but only bishops: by the imposition of their hands it is, that the church giveth power of order, both unto presbyters and deacons.[8]

55.   Nonetheless, there was pressure of invective from Rome and from Puritans and Separatists in England. Some of the more militant Puritans sought to replace episcopal government with presbyterian government, such as that of Calvin's Geneva, regarding bishops not as "pastors, labourers, and watchmen," but as "that swinishe rabble," as "pettie Antichrists, proud prelates, intolerable withstanders of reformation, enemies of the gospel, and most covetous wretched priests."[9]   Indeed, episcopacy was altogether suppressed in the Church of England following the Civil War during the Common-wealth period (1649-1660), but it was restored after the Interregnum. The result of all this controversy, however, was that, rather than merely accepting the threefold order as an historic given, there were now those who began to argue that the historic episcopate was of divine origin and necessary, somewhat in imitation of the Puritans who argued that presbyterian government was of divine origin and necessary. Richard Hooker had argued that the first "institution of bishops could be traced back to Christ himself, through the Apostles," but he was careful to qualify this argument by insisting that episco-pacy was a matter of "positive law." Bishops thus owed "their continued existence in the church since the death of the Apostles to the authority of the church that had chosen to retain them, rather than to any immutable command of divine law."[10] There would be those in the future who would hearken back to Hooker's judicious under-standing, but there would also be those who took a simpler view: Christ instituted bishops, so there must be bishops. The bishops after

the Interregnum of the 17th century insisted on ordaining (or re-ordaining) all ministers previously not episcopally ordained during the Commonwealth period, and the Ordinal of the 1662 Book of Common Prayer as well as the Act of Uniformity in the same year now insisted that episcopal ordination was necessary for the holding of ecclesiastical benefice or admission to the pastoral ministry of the Church of England. Henceforth no one would "be accounted or taken to be a lawful Bishop, Priest, or Deacon" unless he were admitted "according to the form hereafter following, or hath had formerly Episcopal Consecration or Ordination." This requirement applied to ministers from all non-episcopal churches, whether in England or elsewhere. The traditional attitude of the Church of England was nevertheless maintained toward reformed churches elsewhere: they were true churches, whose ministries, though irregular and anomalous, were real and effective.[11] But a clear boundary had been set for the limits of Anglican comprehensiveness that has survived even in the latest (1979) Book of Common Prayer of the Episcopal Church in the United States:

> No persons are allowed to exercise the offices of bishop, priest, or deacon in this Church unless they are so ordained [by "the laying on of episcopal hands"], or have already received such ordination with the laying on of hands by bishops who are themselves duly qualified to confer Holy Orders (preface to the Ordinal, page 510).

56. During the latter half of the 17th century there was thus a shift of theological emphasis in Anglican understandings of episcopacy. Partly this shift was due to the exigencies of polemics, as noted above. It was also stimulated, however, by the rediscovery and authentication of certain patristic texts, especially the first epistle of Clement and the letters of Ignatius. The texts dealt with matters of church order and seemed to indicate a separate and distinct episcopal order from early times.[12] Hence, the episcopal ordering of the church began to be envisaged, in some quarters, not only as historically normative or of divine approbation and apostolic origin (though certainly not as necessary to salvation), but as a divine gift that defines the sphere of covenanted grace and as an apostolic office which is the basis for the Church's authority and identity independent of civil society. One example of this tendency is the bishop of Chester, John Pearson (1673-1686), active in the process of authenticating the genuine letters of Ignatius of Antioch, who became "sure that there can be no power of absolution or authority to consecrate the elements in the Lord's

Supper on the part of one who has not been episcopally ordained."[13]

57.   After this shift in theological emphasis, three ways of understanding episcopacy come to the fore in the following centuries. First were those for whom episcopacy was still a secondary matter. Among many latitudinarians, episcopacy remained a convenient and traditional manner of ordering the ministry. Emerging eighteenth-century Anglican evangelicals largely shared this view with their latitudinarian adversaries. The other two ways of understanding episcopacy, however, accorded it greater theological significance.

58.   The second of these understandings made episcopacy primary. When confronted with latitudinarian theological understandings combined with whig political views of ecclesiastical reformation, the shift of emphasis resulted in the assertion of the Tractarian Movement (1833-1845) that not only was episcopacy of apostolic foundation, but it was necessary to authentic ecclesial life. Appealing to the example and teaching of the early church fathers, such as Cyprian of Carthage, emphasis was placed on the church's self-governance through the episcopate. In Tract 74, for example, it was asserted that non-episcopal forms of ministry, "men thus sending themselves, or sent by we know not whom," have no authority to administer the Sacraments. John Henry Newman (1801-1890) considered bishops to be of the *esse* of the church and urged "the clergy to remember 'the real ground' on which their authority was built, their 'apostolical descent.'" He called upon them "to join with the bishops, and support them in their battle to defend the Church."[14]

59.   A third way of understanding episcopacy, broader but not entirely dissimilar, represents a more comprehensive view resulting from the revolutionary challenges to Christianity coming with the 19th century, yet stemming from the shift in emphasis noted above, and was encouraged by the thought of F. D. Maurice (1805-1872). He commended the institution of the episcopate as "one of the appointed and indispensable signs of a spiritual and universal society,"[15] and he also held that "the main constituent of the Church's polity is the episcopate. Bishops have the direct commission of Christ, as much as did the original holders of the apostolic office."[16] In the case of the Tractarian and Maurician ways of understanding episcopacy, though, the shift of attitude corresponds to a shift in the position of the church in state and society and, as such, informs contemporary discussions

of the episcopate that have been stimulated in part also by the ecumenical movement.

B. ANGLICANISM IN THE AMERICAN CULTURAL CONTEXT

60.   It is remarkable that after the American Revolution colonial Anglicanism survived in the newly founded Protestant Episcopal Church, the first autonomous Anglican Church outside the British Isles but now independent of the civil society. Anglicanism was associated with the tyranny of the British crown, and it might have perished in the United States with the end of British rule. It is also remarkable that the episcopate survived in the new world. There were no resident bishops in colonial Anglicanism and the colonists on the whole had opposed any suggestion of episcopacy, regarding bishops as "proud prelates." The 1789 founding convention of the Episcopal Church met in Philadelphia facing the necessity of resolving widespread differences, principally between those who believed that there could be no discussion of church government without bishops being present and in charge and those who had been prepared to go forward without bishops if for a time the proper consecrations could not be procured, insisting that in this new land it was the faithful people who mattered most. The result was that the historic threefold order of the ordained ministry was continued, though the bishops were elected by both clergy and laity, who were to share in the government of the church in diocesan conventions and in the General Convention.

61.   Although Samuel Seabury, the first bishop of the Episcopal Church in America, and some others like him, maintained a high-church estimation of the vital necessity of episcopacy not only to the church but also to Christian life and salvation, and would have preferred for bishops a greater degree of authority,[17] it was nonetheless determined at the insistence of William White, first bishop of Pennsylvania, that laity were also to participate in every level of church government and even in the selection of those to be ordained. Though reminiscent of conciliar patterns in the early church, such changes in the structure, practice, and understanding of the episcopate were influenced by American colonial experience as well as by the history of the English convocations of Canterbury and York and by a positive theological evaluation of American governmental philosophy and practice, the Articles of Confederation being of particu-

lar influence. Collectively, these arrangements in the Episcopal Church have come to be known as "the constitutional episcopate." The bishop continued to be understood to fulfill a particular and historic ministry within the community of the faithful, but not apart from it.

62. As a result of their new situation, Anglicans in the United States were given further opportunity to explicate their understanding of the historic episcopate. A case in point is the famous Memorial presented to the 1853 General Convention by, among others, William Augustus Muhlenberg, an Episcopal priest whose great-grandfather was the famous Lutheran "patriarch," Henry Melchior Muhlenberg. It petitioned the House of Bishops to take an initiative by ordaining ministers of other traditions (especially on the frontier) without binding them to the Thirty Nine Articles of Religion and the rubrics of the Book of Common Prayer. While the Memorial met with some enthusiasm, no practical action resulted.[18]

C. New Understandings from the Ecumenical Movement

63. Yet as the 19th century progressed, the existence of many competing communions in the U.S.A. caused leaders such as William Reed Huntington to address the issue of church unity. In 1886 the Bishops of the Episcopal Church, meeting in Chicago, appealed to "principles of unity exemplified by the undivided Catholic Church during the first ages of its existence," which they understood to be "essential to the restoration of unity among the divided branches of Christendom." This Chicago-Lambeth Quadrilateral, as it came to be known after it had been affirmed by the 1888 Lambeth Conference (in a slightly amended form), identified four principles "as a basis for an approach to reunion":

a) The Holy Scriptures of the Old and New Testament, as "containing all things necessary to salvation," and as being the rule and ultimate standard of faith.

b) The Apostles' Creed, as the Baptismal Symbol; and the Nicene Creed, as the sufficient statement of the Christian faith.

c) The two Sacraments ordained by Christ Himself—Baptism and the Supper of the Lord—ministered with unfailing use of Christ's words of Institution, and of the elements ordained by Him.

d) The Historic Episcopate, locally adapted in the methods of its administration to the varying needs of the nations and peoples called of
God into the Unity of His Church.[19]

64. It remained for the 20th century ecumenical movement to
multiply conferences and dialogues on matters standing in the way
of visible unity. At times the very instruments of unity have appeared to some as barriers, not least the historic episcopate. The
bishops of the 1920 Lambeth Conference sought to break the impasse
with "An Appeal to All Christian People":

> The vision which rises before us is that of a Church, genuinely
> Catholic, loyal to all truth, and gathering into its fellowship all "who
> profess and call themselves Christians," within whose visible unity
> all the treasures of faith and order, bequeathed as a heritage by the
> past to the present, shall be possessed in common, and made service-
> able to the whole Body of Christ. Within this unity Christian
> Communions now separated from one another would retain much
> that has long been distinctive in their methods of worship and
> service. It is through a rich diversity of life and devotion that the unity
> of the whole fellowship will be fulfilled.[20]

The Appeal was to "an adventure of goodwill and still more of faith,
for nothing less is required than a new discovery of the creative
resources of God." The four principles of unity in the Chicago-
Lambeth Quadrilateral were reworded as follows:

> The Holy Scriptures, as the record of God's revelation of Himself to
> man, and as being the rule and ultimate standard of faith; and the
> Creed commonly called Nicene, as the sufficient statement of the
> Christian faith, and either it or the Apostles' Creed as the Baptismal
> confession of belief;

> The divinely instituted sacraments of Baptism and the Holy Com-
> munion, as expressing for all the corporate life of the whole fellow-
> ship in and with Christ;

> A ministry acknowledged by every part of the Church as possessing
> not only the inward call of the Spirit, but also the commission of
> Christ and the authority of the whole body.[21]

The Appeal addressed the reality of the ordained ministries of
communions without the historic episcopate:

May we not reasonably claim that the Episcopate is the one means of providing such a ministry? It is not that we call in question for a moment the spiritual reality of the ministries of those Communions which do not possess the Episcopate. On the contrary we thankfully acknowledge that these ministries have been manifestly blessed and owned by the Holy Spirit as effective means of grace. But we submit that considerations alike of history and of present experience justify the claim which we make on behalf of the Episcopate. Moreover, we would urge that it is now and will prove to be in the future the best instrument for maintaining the unity and continuity of the Church. But we greatly desire that the office of a Bishop should be everywhere exercised in a representative and constitutional manner. . . .

We believe that for all, the truly equitable approach to union is by way of mutual deference to one another's consciences. To this end, we who send forth this appeal would say that if the authorities of other Communions should so desire, we are persuaded that, terms of union having been otherwise satisfactorily adjusted, Bishops and clergy of our Communion would willingly accept from these authorities a form of commission or recognition which would commend our ministry to their congregations as having its place in the one family life. . . .

It is our hope that the same motive would lead ministers who have not received it to accept a commission through episcopal ordination, as obtaining for them a ministry throughout the whole fellowship.

In so acting no one of us could possibly be taken to repudiate his past ministry. God forbid that any man should repudiate a past experience rich in spiritual blessings for himself and others. Nor would any of us be dishonoring the Holy Spirit of God, Whose call led us all to our several ministries, and Whose power enabled us to perform them. We shall be publicly and formally seeking additional recognition of a new call to wider service in a reunited church, and imploring for ourselves God's grace and strength to fulfill the same.[22]

Thus we have a moving admission of the impoverishment of all ordained ministries by the fact that they are not in communion with each other.

65.   Responses to this Appeal and to like messages from other communions have been deliberate but steady. Notable examples are the unions of Anglican dioceses with Christians of other traditions in the Churches of South India, North India, Pakistan, and Bangladesh.

Discussions have continued in the World Council of Churches Commission on Faith and Order and between communions in many parts of the world, including the Anglican-Lutheran dialogues. Reflection on the experience of steadily widening dialogue, as well as on that of full-communion concordats with the Old Catholic Churches of Europe, the Philippine Independent Church, and the Mar Thoma Church, has led the Episcopal Church to an understanding of the goal of visible unity as "one eucharistic fellowship . . . a communion of Communions."[23] The work of the Consultation on Church Union in the U.S.A. with churches of the Reformed and Methodist traditions has produced a proposal in light of this goal statement which seeks to incorporate the historic episcopate.[24]

66.   The Anglican-Reformed International Commission has produced the report *God's Reign and Our Unity*, which is rich in material concerning the reconciliation of ordained ministries. On the issue of continuity of succession, it declares:

> We have been led to acknowledge . . . the reality of one another's churchly life. But this gives us no ground for concluding that the historic continuity of ordinations is an irrelevance. On the contrary it is an element in the proper visible form of the Church's unity in space and time, to the end of the age and the ends of the earth. We therefore affirm that the ways by which our separated churches are brought into unity must be such as to ensure (a) that the reality of God's gift of ministry to the churches in their separation is unambiguously acknowledged; and (b) that the continuity of succession in ordination with the undivided Church is — so far as lies in our power — visibly restored and maintained.[25]

67.   The Standing Commission on Ecumenical Relations of the Episcopal Church reassessed the relation of the historic episcopate to apostolic succession in light of the ecumenical dialogues, and in 1976 produced what it called a "working statement" which acknowledged that "apostolicity has many strands."[26] This general approach was then formally approved when the 1982 General Convention adopted a resolution on "Principles of Unity" which reaffirmed the Chicago-Lambeth Quadrilateral and in explication thereof broadened the fourth point to embrace the concept of apostolicity:

> Apostolicity is evidenced in continuity with the teaching, the ministry, and the mission of the apostles. Apostolic teaching must, under the guidance of the Holy Spirit, be founded upon the Holy Scriptures

and the ancient fathers and creeds, making its proclamation of Jesus Christ and his Gospel for each new age consistent with those sources, not merely reproducing them in a transmission of verbal identity. Apostolic ministry exists to promote, safeguard and serve apostolic teaching. All Christians are called to this ministry by their Baptism. In order to serve, lead and enable this ministry, some are set apart and ordained in the historic orders of Bishop, Presbyter, and Deacon. We understand the historic episcopate as central to this apostolic ministry and essential to the reunion of the Church, even as we acknowledge "the spiritual reality of the ministries of those Communions which do not possess the Episcopate" (Lambeth Appeal 1920, Section 7). Apostolic mission is itself a succession of apostolic teaching and ministry inherited from the past and carried into the present and future. Bishops in apostolic succession are, therefore, the focus and personal symbols of this inheritance and mission as they preach and teach the Gospel and summon the people of God to their mission of worship and service.[27]

68.   The 1985 General Convention directed Episcopal participants in Lutheran-Episcopal Dialogue III to advocate paragraph 53(a) of *Baptism, Eucharist and Ministry* as "a way forward" toward the mutual recognition of the ordained ministries of our respective churches:

> Churches which have preserved the episcopal succession are asked to recognize both the apostolic content of the ordained ministry which exists in churches which have not maintained such succession and also the existence in these churches of a ministry of *episkope* in various forms.

D. The Prayer Book Teaching on the Episcopate

69.   This review of the ministry of the historic episcopate in the Episcopal Church as a Province of the Anglican Communion may conclude with statements on the meaning of the episcopate taken from the Book of Common Prayer (U.S.A., 1979). "An Outline of the Faith," after identifying the ministers of the Church as "lay persons, bishops, priests, and deacons," each of whom represents Christ in a particular way within the unity of the one Body, describes the ministry of the bishop:

The ministry of a bishop is to represent Christ and his Church, particularly as apostle, chief priest, and pastor of a diocese; to guard the faith, unity, and discipline of the whole Church; to proclaim the Word of God; to act in Christ's name for the reconciliation of the world and the building up of the Church; and to ordain others to continue Christ's ministry.[28]

In the rite for "The Ordination of a Bishop" the presiding bishop addresses the bishop-elect with this description of the episcopal office during the examination before the consecration:

... The people have chosen you and have affirmed their trust in you by acclaiming your election. A bishop in God's holy Church is called to be one with the apostles in proclaiming Christ's resurrection and interpreting the Gospel, and to testify to Christ's sovereignty as Lord of lords and King of kings.

You are called to guard the faith, unity, and discipline of the Church; to celebrate and to provide for the administration of the sacraments of the New Covenant; to ordain priests and deacons and to join in ordaining bishops; and to be in all things a faithful pastor and wholesome example for the entire flock of Christ.

With your fellow bishops you will share in the leadership of the Church throughout the world. Your heritage is the faith of patriarchs, prophets, apostles, and martyrs, and those of every generation who have looked to God in hope. Your joy will be to follow him who came, not to be served, but to serve, and to give his life a ransom for many.[29]

During the Prayer of Consecration the presiding bishop and other bishops lay their hands upon the head of the bishop-elect and say together:

Therefore, Father, make N. a bishop in your Church. Pour out upon *him* the power of your princely Spirit, whom you bestowed upon your beloved Son Jesus Christ, with whom he endowed the apostles, and by whom your Church is built up in every place, to the glory and unceasing praise of your Name.[30]

The "Preface to the Ordination Rites" states the intention and purpose of this church to maintain and continue the threefold ministry:

The Holy Scriptures and ancient Christian writers make it clear that from the apostles' time, there have been different ministries within the Church. In particular, since the time of the New Testament, three distinct orders of ordained ministers have been characteristic of Christ's holy catholic Church. First, there is the order of bishops who carry on the apostolic work of leading, supervising, and uniting the Church. Secondly, associated with them are the presbyters, or ordained elders, in subsequent times generally known as priests. Together with the bishops, they take part in the governance of the Church, in the carrying out of its missionary and pastoral work, and in the preaching of the Word of God and administering his holy Sacraments. Thirdly, there are deacons who assist bishops and priests in all of this work. It is also a special responsibility of deacons to minister in Christ's name to the poor, the sick, the suffering, and the helpless.

The persons who are chosen and recognized by the Church as being called by God to the ordained ministry are admitted to these sacred orders by solemn prayer and the laying on of episcopal hands. It has been, and is, the intention and purpose of this Church to maintain and continue these three orders; and for this purpose these services of ordination and consecration are appointed. No persons are allowed to exercise the offices of bishop, priest, or deacon in this Church unless they are so ordained, or have already received such ordination with the laying on of hands by bishops who are themselves duly qualified to confer Holy Orders.

It is also recognized and affirmed that the threefold ministry is not the exclusive property of this portion of Christ's catholic Church, but is a gift from God for the nurture of his people and the proclamation of his Gospel everywhere. Accordingly, the manner of ordaining in this Church is to be such as has been, and is, most generally recognized by Christian people as suitable for the conferring of the sacred orders of bishop, priest, and deacon.[31]

5

The Gift of Full Communion

A. CONCORDAT OF AGREEMENT

70.   In Chapter 1 we described the historic impasse which has thus far proven to be an impediment to full communion between Lutherans and Anglicans. In Chapter 2 we identified the theological consensus on the gospel, on apostolicity, and on the unity given us in Christ. Chapters 3 and 4 are surveys of Lutheran and Anglican history for the past 450 years. The dialogues have revealed that there have been profound similarities in our 16th century experience, in the type of reforms introduced in different countries associated with our two traditions, in the theological perspectives shared by our 16th century documents. Our studies of these similarities during the three rounds of dialogue over a period of more than two decades have led us to a deepened appreciation for each other's traditions. Dialogues during a great many years, at every level—national, regional, international— have disclosed that our distinctive emphases are complementary: Lutherans with an emphasis on doctrine, Anglicans with an emphasis on worship. We are now ready to propose a Concordat of Agreement between the Episcopal Church and the Evangelical Lutheran Church in America. It is our fervent prayer that the actions proposed in the Concordat of Agreement can be the means by which the Holy Spirit gives both our churches the gift of full communion.

71.   The mandate given to our dialogue is "the discussion of any other outstanding questions that must be resolved before full communion can be established between" our churches. We are using for purposes of the Concordat of Agreement the definition of "full

communion" which has been formulated by the Anglican-Lutheran Joint Working Group, meeting in Cold Ash, Berkshire, England, in 1983.[1] "Full Communion" means that "members of one body may receive the sacraments of the other"; that bishops from each church participate in consecrations of bishops from the other church, "thus acknowledging the duty of mutual care and concern"; that clergy from each church "may exercise liturgical functions in a congregation of the other"; and that there be organs of consultation "to express and strengthen the fellowship and enable common witness, life and service." We cannot emphasize strongly enough the following three convictions with regard to "full communion."

72.   (1) The unity which is expressed by the term "full communion" is not something we achieve by processes of dialogue or by legislative agreements. It is a gift which we receive in and from Christ, who has reconciled all of humanity to God "in one body through the cross" (Eph. 2:16), who has made us one through our baptism into him (Gal. 3:26-28). "The unity of the church is given, not achieved. The church can only be one because it is constituted by the gospel in word and sacrament, and there is but one gospel" (*Implications of the Gospel*, Par. 98).

73.   (2) The unity which is expressed by the term "full communion" is not intended merely to facilitate the convenience of communicants and clergy. It is intended above all to express the fully shared life and mission of our churches. When the church hears together the one gospel and feasts together at the one table of the Messiah, it is given the gift of life and mission. In the midst of the debilitating and destructive sense of fragmentation and homelessness which often accompanies a pluralistic and rootless culture, every experience of unity which Christ gives his disciple community is a witness. Moreover, the unity of Christ's disciples is received in the midst of as well as for the sake of his mission in the world. Hence both unity and mission are given in and with the gospel.

> The *gift* of Christ is that he sends his disciples as he has been sent (John 20:21), that they are to witness to God's forgiving judgement and verdict by setting at liberty all who are in the bondage of sin, that they are to witness to God's confounding and defeat of evil by unmasking the demonic powers and joining the struggle against them. . . . In Christ the Church is called to be a sign, an instrument and a foretaste of the kingdom of God. The Church awakens to the astonishing

discovery that its mission is a gift, that it has indeed been given the pearl of great price, the treasure hidden in a field (Matt. 13:44-46) and that this discovery is the reason for gathering others in order to participate in the joy (Luke 15:8-10).[2]

74.   (3) The unity which is expressed by the term "full communion" is, in part, received and expressed in the interchangeability and reciprocity of ordained ministries. "I planted, Apollos watered, but God gave the growth. So neither he who plants nor he who waters is anything, but only God who gives the growth. He who plants and he who waters are equal . . ." (I Cor. 3:6-8; cf. Gal. 2:7-10). The church which becomes visible when it is gathered by the gospel in Word and Sacrament requires the gift of ministries for the proclamation of the Word and the administration of the Sacraments. Such ministries have been given by Christ for building up his body "until we all attain to the unity of the faith" (Eph. 4:11-13). The collegiality of the ordained ministries of the church is given in and for the sake of the unity and mission of the gospel (I Cor. 12:4—14:33).

75.   We are aware of the fact that our churches have had different histories with regard to ordained ministries since the differing reforms of the 16th century and the differing experiences of our churches in the United States.[3] We are also aware that within each of our churches there are differences of both interpretation and tradition with regard to many aspects of the ordained ministry. We do not believe that "full communion" means the elimination of all of these differences. Both of our churches live with internal diversity of traditions. At Cold Ash, the Anglican-Lutheran Joint Working Group agreed that

> to be in full communion means that churches become interdependent while remaining autonomous. One is not elevated to be the judge of the other nor can it remain insensitive to the other; neither is each body committed to every secondary feature of the tradition of the other. . . .Full communion should not imply the suppressing of ethnic, cultural or ecclesial characteristics of traditions which may in fact be maintained and developed by diverse institutions within one communion.[4]

The purpose of the Concordat of Agreement which we are proposing to our churches is to commit ourselves to the cultivation of just those common forms which will facilitate the maximum reciprocity and interchangeability of ordained ministry.

76. In drafting the Concordat of Agreement which we are proposing to our churches we have been assisted by *The Niagara Report* of the Anglican-Lutheran International Continuation Committee (ALICC). In 1983, the Anglican-Lutheran Joint Working Group, authorized by the Anglican Consultative Council and the Lutheran World Federation, recommended the establishment of a permanent international Continuation Committee. This committee was given as its first mandate the convening of an international Anglican-Lutheran consultation on *episkope*. The consultation took place at Niagara Falls, Ontario, in September, 1987. The Continuation Committee then issued a report with a series of recommendations to Anglican and Lutheran churches which grew out of the consultation. The recommendation addressed to churches of the Anglican Communion was as follows:

> Anglican Churches should make the necessary canonical revisions so that they can acknowledge and recognize the full authenticity of the existing ministries of Lutheran Churches.[5]

The 1988 Lambeth Conference welcomed *The Niagara Report*, and commended it "to the member Churches of the Anglican Communion for study and synodical reception." Lambeth also asked the Continuation Committee (now the Anglican-Lutheran International Commission) "to explore more thoroughly the theological and canonical requirements that are necessary in both Churches to acknowledge and recognize the full authenticity of existing ministries." Member Churches of the Anglican Communion are urged "to move towards the fullest possible ecclesial recognition and the goal of full communion" with Lutheran churches.[6] Likewise the Eighth Assembly of the Lutheran World Federation, meeting in Curitiba, Brazil, from January 30 to February 8, 1990, "expressed its joy" at this action taken by the 1988 Lambeth Conference, and resolved that the Lutheran World Federation should "renew its commitment to the goal of full communion with the churches of the Anglican Communion; and . . . urge LWF member Churches to take appropriate steps toward its realization." At the heart of *The Niagara Report* is an action proposed to each church. If the Episcopal Church can respond positively to the Lambeth resolution which recognizes "the presence of the Church of Jesus Christ in the Lutheran Communion as in our own" and take the canonical steps necessary to recognize the full authenticity of existing ministries of the Evangelical Lutheran Church in America, then the way is open for the Evangelical Lutheran Church in America *simultaneously* to take the equally significant steps to return to the traditional polity (the "historic episcopate") which is affirmed in its confessional documents (cf. paras. 36-41 above), to accept the sign of historic succession for its bishops in the future. Both churches have reason to remember the statement of Archbishop Robert Runcie that "it is dangerous to pray for unity because God is answering our prayers. Doors are opened and we stand wondering if we should enter."[7]

77.   We believe that our two churches can enter into the Concordat of Agreement which we propose because of the common confession of the gospel which we share and which we have sought to express in all of our previous dialogue reports. We have also discovered that we share a sufficient common understanding of episcopal ministry, both in future vision[8] and in the past histories of our separate churches, over which we have not officially disagreed nor exchanged invective in the past. Each of us has been and is engaged in extensive dialogue on ordained ministry with other churches with whom we have disagreed about it, such as with the Roman Catholic Church and (in and outside the Consultation on Church Union) with the Methodist churches and with churches of the Reformed tradition. Much progress has been made in the overcoming of past disputes on this point in these dialogues, and we are resolved that they shall continue and that any measure of unity we achieve among ourselves shall also serve as a vehicle for rapprochement with them.[9]   In our proposed Concordat of Agreement we agree to respect the full communion (pulpit and altar fellowship) with those churches which each of our churches already has. We look forward to possible joint dialogues with other churches in the future. But to our two particular churches, Lutheran and Anglican, the freedom for reconciliation of ministry in mission is being given now.

78.   We wish to make clear at this point what will take place if our churches enter into the proposed Concordat of Agreement and some of the meaning of what will take place. As an expression of our communion, all persons newly elected to the office of bishop in both churches will be jointly consecrated by at least three bishops from each of our churches. No bishops already in office will be reconsecrated or re-ordained. Nor will any ordained presbyters (priests/pastors) from either church be re-ordained. Both churches agree to recognize the full authenticity of existing ministries. Nothing will be done which calls into question the authenticity of present ordinations

and ministries and sacraments. Lutherans also need to understand that the future joint consecrations do not mean that Lutheran bishops will have greater authority, for the gospel of God's promise confers all the authority which the church and its ministers have or need. Nor will future Lutheran bishops have powers which they do not now have. They will continue to exercise *episkope* on the basis of the framework of constitutional accountability which currently obtains in the Evangelical Lutheran Church in America. Canon law in the Episcopal Church and synodical constitutions in the Evangelical Lutheran Church in America will continue to set terms of office and procedures for the election of bishops. But the Concordat of Agreement envisions those changes which will eventuate in a common *collegium* of bishops. The meaning of the joint consecration of future bishops is that the bishop is to serve as sign and means of unity between the local and the universal dimensions of the church. The meaning of episcopal succession is that the bishop is to serve as a sign and means of unity between the church in the present and its continuity with the church of the past and the future.[10]

79.   We believe that our churches are free to consider and to make the changes called for in the proposed Concordat of Agreement because of the authority of the gospel itself. The authority of the gospel is identified early in the synoptic Gospels. There the authority of Jesus is contrasted with that of the scribes (cf. Mark 1:22 and parallels). Jesus' authority was eschatological, that is, it was based on the present and future Reign of God. He was crucified in an intended negative judgment upon his implicit and explicit messianic claims. The resurrection of Jesus implies a dramatic reversal of this judgment. Indeed, because he can no longer be inhibited by death, the risen Messiah of Matthew's Gospel can make a sweeping and powerful claim: "All authority in heaven and on earth has been given to me" (Matt. 28:18).

80.   Thus Jesus, himself, distinguishes between authority which comes from the gospel's promise and authority which comes only from fidelity to the way things are and have been (Mark 2:27-28; 7:1-23; Matt. 8:20-29). Authority which comes only from the past is slavishly dependent upon precedent and is bound to the *status quo*. It serves those who already have power, those who already have a stake in the way things are. But authority which comes from the gospel's promise creates new opportunities, gives new hope to those who are otherwise hopeless, to those who are excluded from the

future by oppression and evil, by sickness and sin. The authority of the gospel's promise is grounded in the eschatological life, death, and resurrection of Jesus.[11] It is thus shaped by the history of Jesus which reveals both the way and the destiny of the church. Faith in the gospel involves the church in risks when it acts on the basis of Jesus' promise. For its authority to worship and to witness is the authority of what will finally be when the Kingdom of God is consummated. It is the authority which comes from anticipating the future because Jesus alone has the power to determine the destiny of the world and of all of humanity.[12] It is this authority of promise which gives authority to the Bible, the catholic creeds, and the confessional and liturgical books of the church, as well as to all structures and offices of ministry in the church. This authority is able to reform and renew the church as well as to give life to the dead and to call into existence that which does not exist (e.g., Romans 4:13-25).

81. This understanding of authority has contributed to the ability of our churches to ordain women to the presbyterate/pastorate and to the episcopate. This is evidence that Episcopalians take seriously the provision of the Lambeth Quadrilateral that the historic episcopate can be "locally adapted" from the perspective of the gospel. It is also evidence that the Evangelical Lutheran Church in America is willing and able to understand the episcopate as subject to the gospel, a point also endorsed by Episcopalians. On this basis of authority, our churches are also able to take the responsible risks through which we will be given full communion with each other. We will be able to live with reasonable anomalies and ambiguities for some short time as we await the consummation or complete realization of the gift of full communion. For the gospel of the Kingdom of God calls the churches to risk all the gifts they have been given in answer to God's call to discipleship (cf. Matthew 25:14-30), to risk all the gifts they have been given in response to God's call to unity (John 17:14-26). The church is called here and now to anticipate, in its very being the coming and promised ideal of the Kingdom of God.[13]

B. Toward Full Communion

82. In the period since the Episcopal Church and the Evangelical Lutheran Church in America have entered into the Agreement of 1982 our churches have built upon our recognition of each other as "Churches in which the Gospel is preached and taught." Our churches have begun to discover that in each other's churches there

exists a sustained and serious commitment to the apostolic mission of the Church. We have begun to cultivate the common discipleship to which we have been called in one body, by one Spirit, through one baptism, thankful to the one Lord, our Savior Jesus Christ, in whom we have received one faith, one hope, "one God and Father of us all, who is above all and through all and in all" (Eph. 4:3-6). In the eucharists jointly celebrated under the provisions of Interim Sharing of the Eucharist we have already begun to experience that unity and *koinonia* of eschatological promise which is anticipated in every celebration of the eucharist.[14]

83.   We are grateful to God for the gift of *episkope* which has been given to each of our churches, although in different forms. We acknowledge in each other's ministries of *episkope* the fruits of the presence of Jesus Christ and the activity of the Holy Spirit: the offering of sacrifices of praise and thanksgiving, the reflection of the faithful love of God towards the world, care for the nurture and growth of all the faithful, commitment to the breaking in of the Kingdom of God in justice and peace for the whole earth.

84.   We recognize, however, that the ministries of *episkope* which we have received in each of our churches do not incontestably link our churches to the *koinonia* of the wider Church of God on earth throughout time and place. We confess to God, to each other, and to all Christian people how far, in our discharge of the ministry of *episkope*, our Churches have fallen short of the unity and continuity of the apostolic commission to which we are called. We ask of each other forgiveness for our disregard of each other's gifts, for our lack of humility, and for our past toleration of our division.

85.   We earnestly desire to remove those barriers which prevent the life of our churches from reflecting the unity of heart and mind which is God's gift to the people of God. We commit ourselves to whatever is required of us to reach a common mind as to how the mission of the people of God can most fruitfully be served in every place, so that there may be united witness to the gospel, in word and deed, and a common enjoyment of the means of grace. We intend thereby also to promote the unity of all churches with whom we are seeking, or have already discovered, agreement in the one faith of the church catholic.

86.   We rejoice in rediscovering in each other our common inheritance of faith and of life. We rejoice in our unity in the One, Holy,

Catholic, and Apostolic Church. "Praise be to the God and Father of our Lord Jesus Christ, who has bestowed on us in Christ every spiritual blessing in the heavenly realms" (Eph. 1:3).

87.   We are agreed that the unity and mission of the gospel frees us for more than a simplistic recognition of each other's ministries of diocesan/synodical and parochial/congregational leadership. Authentic recognition involves the interaction and integration of leadership, especially that of *episkope*, for purposes of common life and mission. Such interaction and integration for purposes of life and mission means receiving the gift of comparable, compatible, and interchangeable forms of *episkope*. As this Report demonstrates, both of our churches have already experienced change and development in the forms and understanding of *episkope* throughout our respective histories. Now new developments are being given to both of us. We cannot, therefore, commend uncritically either the appropriation of the historic episcopate as it has developed in the Episcopal Church or the perpetuation of the exercise of *episkope* as it has developed in the Evangelical Lutheran Church in America.[15]

88.   Neither of our churches claims such a degree of faithfulness to our calling by the apostolic gospel, that is, a continuity in either doctrine or order, as would enable either to sit in judgment on the other. Nevertheless both of our churches have been given by God such faithfulness to the apostolic gospel that today we can recognize each other as sister churches.

89.   The Episcopal Church and the Evangelical Lutheran Church in America have received, and can affirm together, as gifts for unity, the canonical Scriptures, the creeds and conciliar decisions of the ancient church, the reforms of the 16th century (especially in confessional writings such as *The Book of Concord*), the liturgical tradition of the church (especially the Book of Common Prayer), and the continuity of the ordained ministry through which the Word of God has been preached and the sacraments and other rites of the Church have been administered. The question of the historic episcopate through which clergy have been ordained, something which has been divisive between us, we believe we have transcended in the Concordat of Agreement attached to this report.

90.   Formal recognition of each other's ministries so that our churches acknowledge a relationship of full communion between them cannot

simply mean that neither church changes. Nor can it mean that either church changes merely to meet the expectations and requirements of the other. Rather both of our churches are being called to acknowledge that the experience and practice of full communion will involve us both *simultaneously* in changes and commitment to reforms. The simultaneity of the actions of our churches means that we trust each other as churches, that neither church requires prior conditions of the other, and that both churches are willing to make changes for the sake of unity.

91.   The *simultaneous* actions which our churches offer each other can facilitate the continuing renewal of the episcopate as a pastoral office engaged in transmitting effectively the apostolic faith, in leading the church in its mission, and furthering the worldwide restoration of church unity on a basis that is ecumenical, evangelical, and catholic.

The Epiphany of Our Lord
January 6, 1991

Notes

Introduction

1. *Lutheran-Episcopal Dialogue: A Progress Report* (Cincinnati: Forward Movement Publications, 1972), p. 24. Lutheran participants in the dialogue were The Rev. O. V. Anderson, co-chair, Prof. Sidney E. Ahlstrom, Prof. Wendell W. Frerichs, The Rev. Paul M. Hasvold, The Rev. Paul Jacobs, Prof. Robert W. Jenson, Prof. Peter Kjeseth, Prof. Fred Meuser, Prof. Carl S. Meyer, The Rev. Norman Nagel, The Rev. Paul D. Opsahl (staff), and The Rev. William G. Rusch (staff). Episcopal participants were The Rt. Rev. Richard S. M. Emrich, co-chair, Prof. Reginald Fuller, The Very Rev. Harvey H. Guthrie, Jr., The Rev. John W. Hildebrand, The Very Rev. J. Ogden Hoffmann, Jr., Prof. Jean Henkel Johnson, Prof. John H. Rodgers, Jr., The Rev. Robert H. Whitaker, and Peter Day (staff).

2. *Lutheran-Episcopal Dialogue: Report and Recommendations* (Cincinnati: Forward Movement Publications, 1981). Reprinted in William A. Norgren, editor, *What Can We Share?* A Lutheran-Episcopal Resource and Study Guide (Cincinnati: Forward Movement Publications, 1985), pp. 38-59. Lutheran participants in the dialogue were The Rev. Robert I. Wietelmann, co-chair, The Rev. Carl L. Bornmann, The Rev. Stephen Bremer, Prof. Robert J. Goeser, The Rev. Jerald C. Joersz, The Rev. Norman Nagel, Prof. Ralph Quere, Prof. Frank Senn, The Rev. Richard L. Trost, The Rev. Cyril Wismar, Sr.,,The Rev. Paul Opsahl (staff), and The Rev. Joseph A. Burgess (staff). Episcopal participants were The Rt. Rev. William G. Weinhauer, co-chair, Prof. Reginald H. Fuller, The Very Rev. J. Ogden Hoffman, Jr., Prof. William H. Petersen, Prof. J. Howard Rhys, The Very Rev. John H. Rodgers, Jr., Prof. Louis Weil, Dr. Peter Day (staff), and The Rev. William A. Norgren (staff).

3. *Journal of the General Convention, The Episcopal Church, 1982*, pp. C-47 - C-48. *Report of the Convention of the Lutheran Church in America, 1982*, pp. 182 and 266; *Report of the Convention of the American Lutheran Church, 1982*, pp. 975-976; *Proceedings of the Fourth Delegate Assembly of the Association of Evangelical Lutheran Churches*, September 7-9, 1982, pp. 15-16. Cf. Norgren, *What Can We Share?* pp. 6-8. There are some variations in the use of capital letters between the resolution adopted by The Episcopal Church and the resolutions adopted by the three Lutheran churches. This resolution was reaffirmed at the constituting convention of The Evangelical Lutheran Church in America, uniting the American Lutheran Church, the Association of Evangelical Lutheran Churches, and the Lutheran Church in America in 1987. Cf. *Minutes:* Evangelical Lutheran Church in America Constituting Convention, April 30 — May 3, 1987, Resolutions ELCA 87.30.17 and ELCA 87.30.19, pp. 28-30.

4. D. S. Armentrout, "Lutheran-Episcopal Conversations in the Nineteenth Century," *Historical Magazine of the Protestant Episcopal Church*, Vol. 44, No. 2 (1975), pp. 167-187, esp. pp. 181ff.

5. Louis A. Haselmayer, "The Church of Sweden and the Anglican Communion," *The Holy Cross Magazine*, Vol. 60, No. 8 (August 1949), pp. 213-222. See also *The Church of England and the Church of Sweden: Report of the Commission Appointed by the Archbishop of Canterbury* (Mowbray, 1911); "The Reply of the Bishops of the Church of Sweden to the Resolutions of the Lambeth Conference of 1920. April 1922," in *Documents on Christian Unity 1920-4*, edited by G. K. A. Bell, 1924; *The Church of England and the Church of Finland: A Summary of the Proceedings at the Conferences held*

in 1933 and 1934 (S.P.C.K., 1934); also reprinted in *Documents on Christian Unity, 1930-1948*, edited by G. K. A. Bell; *Record of a Conference between the Commission of Comity of the Evangelical Lutheran Augustana Synod and the Sub-Committee of the Joint Commission for Conference on Church Unity of the Protestant Episcopal Church, held at Evanston, Illinois, December 3-4, 1935*, typewritten manuscript in the libraries of the General Theological Seminary, New York City, and Nashotah House, Nashotah, Wisconsin (Evanston, 1936); *Conferences between Representatives Appointed by the Archbishop of Canterbury on Behalf of the Church of England and Representatives of the Evangelical Lutheran Churches of Latvia and Estonia* (S.P.C.K., 1938); and *The Church of England and the Churches of Norway, Denmark and Iceland: Report of a Committee Appointed by the Archbishop of Canterbury in 1951* (S.P.C.K., 1952).

6. Todd W. Nichol, "The Augustana Synod and Episcopacy," *Lutheran Quarterly*, Vol. III, No. 2 (Summer 1989), pp. 156-159.

7. Available through Augsburg Fortress, Publishers, Minneapolis, and Forward Movement Publications, Cincinnati.

8. *From Dar es Salaam to Budapest 1977-1984*, LWF Report No. 17/18 (April 1984), p. 22. Cf. p. 211.

9. The text of the Cold Ash Report is in William A. Norgren, editor, *What Can We Share?*, *op.cit.*, pp. 85-94.

10. *Ibid.*, pp. 26-27.

11. *Budapest 1984, Proceedings of the Seventh Assembly*, "In Christ—Hope for the World," LWF Report No. 19/20 (February 1985), p. 216.

12. *Bonds of Affection: Proceedings of the Anglican Consultative Council — 6, Badagry, Nigeria, 1984*, p. 101.

13. *The Truth Shall Make You Free: The Lambeth Conference 1988*, pp. 204-206.

14. Minutes of the Executive Committee, The Lutheran World Federation, July 31-August 9, 1989, p. 21.

15. *Proceedings of the Eighth Assembly of the Lutheran World Federation*, LWF Report No. 28/29 (December 1990), p. 107.

16. *Many Voices One Song, 1989 Churchwide Assembly, Evangelical Lutheran Church in America*, Reports and Records, Vol. 2, pp. 423, 432-433.

17. *Ecumenism: The Vision of the Evangelical Lutheran Church in America* (Chicago: Office for Ecumenical Affairs, ELCA, 1989), p. 14. This is from No. 3 of the listing of some of the characteristics of full communion.

Chapter 1: The Historic Impasse

1. For a survey of these see J. Robert Wright, editor, *Quadrilateral at One Hundred* (Cincinnati: Forward Movement Publications, 1988), pp. 8-46.

2. Texts and references in Wright, *op. cit.*, pp. 41-42.

3. *LED I* (1972), p. 161, Par. 87.

4. *LED II* (1981), p. 16.

5. *Ibid.*, p. 21.

6. *Ibid.*, p. 162, Par. 89.

7. Report on "The Historic Episcopate," Division of Studies, LCUSA (New York, 1984), p. 6. The participants in the study were Prof. Paul S. Berge, Prof. Karl P. Donfried, The Rev. Jerrold A. Eickmann, The Rev. Gary E. Glithvedt, Prof. Robert J. Goeser, The Rev. Samuel H. Nafzger, The Rev. James Pragman, The Rev. William G. Rusch, Prof. James L. Schaaf, The Rev. Edward D. Schneider, Prof. John H. Tietjen, The Rev. Wilson E. Touhsaent, The Rev. William C. Weinrich, and The Rev. Joseph A. Burgess. Berge, Goeser, Rusch, and Schneider are members of LED III; Burgess was the LCUSA staff member for LED III until the end of 1987.

8. *LED I*, pp. 135-136. It is most important to add that the paper continued with the following paragraph:

I do not see that the matter should be hopeless. As to the theology of the matter, it seems to me we have some progress. If the understanding arrived at in our last meeting is indeed satisfactory to both denominations, Lutherans should be happy. For the Lutheran position means that so long as the episcopacy—or any other "ceremony"—is not made an antecedent condition of communion, Lutherans are committed to limitless openness thereafter, both in investigating the inadequacy of their own previous arrangements and in achieving new arrangements for future forms of the church. The explicit recognition of "episcope" as an intrinsic function in the church has not been characteristic of Lutheranism; but it in no way violates Lutheran principle, and merely makes up a rather obvious lacuna in our thought. If some such statements as those achieved in our previous meeting could be adopted by an authoritative entity in each denomination, we would be past the point theologically sticky for Lutherans. Nor need Lutherans demand that this be the *only* statement on episcopacy in force in either denomination.

9. Statement on "The Unity We Seek," adopted by the Lutheran World Federation Assembly at Budapest in 1984. See *Budapest 1984*, p. 175. The entire statement is quoted in the ELCA statement, "Ecumenism: The Vision of the Evangelical Lutheran Church in America," reprinted in *A Commentary on "Ecumenism: The Vision of the ELCA"* (Minneapolis: Augsburg, 1990). See pp. 40-41.

10. *Papers of the Consultation*: Background for *The Niagara Report*, Geneva, 1987, p. 16.

11. J. Robert Wright, "Martin Luther: An Anglican Ecumenical Appreciation," *Anglican and Episcopal History*, Vol. 56, No. 3 (September 1987), especially pp. 325-326.

12. Full text in *Journal of the General Convention, The Episcopal Church*, 1985, p. 445, and in *Ecumenical Bulletin* No. 71 (May-June 1985), p. 35.

13. George A. Lindbeck, "Episcopacy and the Unification of the Churches: Two Approaches," in *Promoting Unity*, edited by H. George Anderson and James R. Crumley Jr. (Minneapolis: Augsburg, 1989), pp. 53-54.

14. Paragraph 28. Full text in *Ecumenical Trends*, Vol. 17, No. 9 (October 1988), pp. 137-143.

15. Lindbeck, *op.cit.*, p. 52

Chapter 2: Theological Consensus

1. Werner Elert, *Abendmahl und Kirchengemeinschaft in der alten Kirche hauptsaechlich des Ostens* (Berlin: Lutherisches Verlagshaus, 1954), p. 90. Cf. the translation by N. E. Nagel, *Eucharist and Church Fellowship in the First Four Centuries* (St. Louis: Concordia Publishing House, 1966), p. 109, and the summary of Elert's classic analysis in Eugene Brand, *Toward a Lutheran Communion: Pulpit and Altar Fellowship*, LWF Report No. 26 (Geneva: The Lutheran World Federation, 1988), pp. 17-19. Other literature on the subject includes F. J. Hort, *The Christian Ecclesia* (London and New York: MacMillan and Co., 1897), John Knox, *The Early Church and the Coming Great Church* (London: Epworth Press, 1957), Stephen Benko, *The Meaning of Sanctorum Communio* (Naperville, Alex R. Allenson, 1964), Jerome Hamer, O.P., *The Church Is a Communion* (London: Geoffrey Chapman, 1964), Hans von Campenhausen, *Ecclesiastical Authority and Spiritual Power in the Church of the First Three Centuries* (Stanford: Stanford University Press, 1969), Ludwig Hertling, S.J., *Communion: Church and Papacy in Early Christianity*, transl. Jared Wicks, S.J. (Chicago: Loyola University Press, 1972), Kenneth Hein, *Eucharist and Excommunication: A Study in Early Christian Doctrine and Discipline* (Frankfurt: Peter Lang, 1973), and Maurice Wiles, "Sacramental Unity in the Early Church," in *Church Membership and Intercommunion*, edited by John Kent and Robert Murray (London: Darton, Longman and Todd, 1973).

2. *LED I* (1972), pp. 14-22.

3. *LED II* (1981), pp. 22-43.

4. A similar summary appears in the bilingual Meissen Statement (1988) adopted by the Church of England and the Evangelical Church of Germany, *Auf dem Weg zu sichtbarer Einheit (On the Way to Visible Unity)*, pp. 16-19.

5. *LED I* (1972), pp. 20-22.
6. Full text in *Journal of the General Convention, The Episcopal Church*, 1976, pp. AA-75 -
   AA-76, in *Ecumenical Bulletin* 17 (May-June 1976), pp. 8-11, and in *Ecumenical Trends*
   Vol. 5, No. 10 (November 1976), pp. 154-156.
7. *LED II* (1981), pp. 31-53.
8. *Ibid.*, p. 40.
9. Michael Root, *"The Niagara Report*: A Possible Lutheran-Anglican Future?" *Dialog*,
   Vol. 28, No. 4 (Autumn 1989), p. 300.
10. L. William Countryman, "The Gospel and the Institutions of the Church With Par-
    ticular Reference to the Historic Episcopate," *Anglican Theological Review*, Vol. LXVI,
    No. 4 (1984), pp. 402-415.
11. *Ibid.*, p. 412.
12. Richard Norris regards this attitude as the first phase in the development of Anglican
    thought and practice with regard to churches *outside of England* whose ministries
    were not episcopally ordained. Prior to 1662, he writes, "the legitimacy of non-
    episcopal orders in foreign Churches was conceded on the precise ground of
    'necessity', that is, on the ground that such Churches had in practice been compelled
    to make a choice—between reformation according to scriptural norms of doctrine
    and practice on the one hand, and, on the other, retention of episcopacy.... Hence
    (the Anglican divines of the seventeenth century) commanded episcopal ordering of
    the Church at home (for domestic dissenters could make no claim of 'necessity') and
    commended it abroad, acknowledging their fellowship with Reformed Churches
    overseas." Richard A. Norris, "Episcopacy," in *The Study of Anglicanism*, edited by
    Stephen Sykes and John Booty (Philadelphia: Fortress Press, 1988), p. 304. See also
    Norman Sykes, *Old Priest and New Presbyter* (Cambridge, 1956), and Paul F.
    Bradshaw, *The Anglican Ordinal* (London, 1971), Chapter 6.
13. *Ibid.*, p. 414.
14. *Ibid.*
15. Paul Berge, "A Response to Bill Countryman's paper, 'The Gospel and the Institu-
    tions of the Church'" (Unpublished Paper, Lutheran-Episcopal Dialogue III, June 10-
    13, 1984), p. 1
16. *Ibid.*, p. 2.
17. *Ibid.*, p. 5
18. *Ibid.*
19. *Ibid.*, p. 6.
20. William Countryman, "The Historic Episcopate: Further Reflections," Unpublished
    Paper, Lutheran-Episcopal Dialogue, June 1989, pp. 5-6.
21. "For Lutherans, the preservation of the Reformation heritage is vital. Anglicans have
    no objection to this; indeed, we see it as embodied in our existing ministry. If
    Lutherans feel it is insufficiently evident, they should help us see how to make it
    more so. For Lutherans themselves, the main issue may be how to ensure against any
    impression that existing orders are being abandoned in favor of something called
    'historic episcopate'. Such abandonment might raise questions about the integrity of
    church life in the past, which would be a betrayal of blessings received and must
    surely be rejected. Accordingly, it is vital that any change in Lutheran rites of
    ordination should emphasize that continuity with the Reformation successions is
    not being broken. This could be done partly with a preface to the ordinal, identifying
    the distinct strands of succession that are being brought together, partly by bringing
    in the historic episcopate from Lutheran sources rather than or in addition to
    Anglican ones, partly by clearly limiting the new ordinal to use for new ordinations.
    Lutherans already have asserted, in the *Confessio Augustana*, the right of a gospel
    ministry of word and sacrament to ignore or circumvent those bishops who oppose
    its work. This, too, would act to preserve a Reformation perspective on the relativity
    of bishops." Countryman, *Ibid.*, pp. 7-8.
22. J. N. D. Kelly, *Early Christian Creeds* (New York: David McKay Company, Ind., 1960),
    pp. 10-13.

23. Cf. L. William Countryman, "Tertullian and the Regula Fidei," *The Second Century* 2 (1982), pp. 208-227; see also J. N. D. Kelly, *op. cit.*, pp. 62-99, 205-230, and 368-397.
24. Robert Jenson, "Baptism," in Carl Braaten and Robert Jenson, editors, *Christian Dogmatics*, Vol. 2 (Philadelphia: Fortress Press, 1984), pp. 326-333.
25. This has come to be the standard account of the development of our liturgies. See such textbooks as *The Study of Liturgy*, ed. by Cheslyn Jones, Geoffrey Wainwright, and Edward Yarnold (New York: Oxford University Press, 1978), pp. 147-208.
26. Cf. Hans von Campenhausen, *Ecclesiastical Authority and Spiritual Power in the Church of the First Three Centuries* (London: Adam and Charles Black, 1969), pp. 149-177; Robert M. Grant, *Augustus to Constantine* (New York: Harper and Row, 1970), pp. 63-68, 145-160.
27. *Baptism, Eucharist and Ministry*, Faith and Order Paper 111 (Geneva: World Council of Chruches, 1982), M. 19-20.
28. "The Chicago-Lambeth Quadrilateral of 1886-88," Book of Common Prayer, p. 878. Cf. "Formula of Concord," VII, 74-84, *The Book of Concord*, pp. 583-584.
29. "The Chicago-Lambeth Quadrilateral of 1886-88," *op. cit.* Cf. Chapter III, B, below, for the Lutheran version of episcopacy "locally adapted."

Chapter 3: The Lutheran Churches and Episcopal Ministry

1. The regional histories are presented in Ivar Asheim and Victor Gold, editors, *Episcopacy in the Lutheran Church?* (Philadelphia: Fortress Press, 1970). For an Anglican evaluation of the continental development cf. J. Robert Wright, "Martin Luther: An Anglican Ecumenical Appreciation," *op.cit.*, pp. 323-325.
2. Wilhelm Maurer, *Historical Commentary on the Augsburg Confession*, tr. by H. George Anderson (Philadelphia: Fortress Press, 1986), p. 15.
3. The Babylonian Captivity of the Church," *Luther's Works*, American Edition (hereafter cited as LW), Vol. 36 (Philadelphia: Fortress Press, 1959), pp. 106-117. "Therefore this 'sacrament' of ordination, if it is anything at all, is nothing else than a certain rite whereby one is called to the ministry of the church. Furthermore, the priesthood is properly nothing but the ministry of the Word—the Word, I say; not the law, but the gospel. And the diaconate is the ministry, not of reading the Gospel or the Epistle, as is the present practice, but of distributing the church's aid to the poor, so that the priests may be relieved of the burden of temporal matters and may give themselves more freely to prayer and the Word. ... Whoever, therefore, does not know or preach the gospel is not only no priest or bishop, but he is a kind of pest to the church." Page 116. See however Apology XIII:11-12, which states, "If ordination is interpreted in relation to the ministry of the Word, we have no objection to calling ordination a sacrament. The ministry of the Word has God's command and glorious promises. . .. If ordination is interpreted this way, we shall not object either to calling the laying on of hands a sacrament."
4. The 1979 Book of Common Prayer, p. 872. Article XXV reads in part: "Those five commonly called sacraments, that is to say, Confirmation, Penance, Orders, Matrimony, and Extreme Unction, are not to be counted for Sacraments of the Gospel, being such as have grown partly of the corrupt following of the Apostles, partly are states of life allowed in the Scriptures; but yet have not like nature of Sacraments with Baptism, and the Lord's Supper, for that they have not any visible sign or ceremony ordained of God." This is cited simply to indicate that Martin Luther's views were widely shared by other reforming traditions in the 16th century.
5. LW, Vol. 40, p. 11. "For the time being I will concede the papal ordinations whereby those whom they call priests are anointed and appointed by the authority of the bishop alone without any consent or election by the people over whom they are to be placed."
6. Cf. Robert Goeser, "Word, Ministry, and Episcopacy according to the Confessions," *The Lutheran Quarterly*, Vol. IV, No. 1 (Spring 1990), p. 51.

7. Eric Gritsch, "Episcopacy: The Legacy of the Lutheran Confessions," Unpublished Paper, Lutheran-Episcopal Dialogue III, June 17-20, 1990, p. 20.

8. Cf. Peter Brunner, *Nikolaus von Amsdorf als Bischof von Naumburg* (Guetersloh: Guetersloher Verlagshaus Gerd Mohn, 1961).

9. This is similar to the role of the "godly prince" in England described by Richard Norris, "Episcopacy," *op. cit.*, p. 297.

10. *Episcopacy in the Lutheran Church?*, p. 65.

11. Richard Norris describes the problems and distortions attendant upon similar development in England. The life of the church "was openly subjected to the secular, civil authority of Parliament; and its bishops, whose votes in the House of Lords had become necessary to the continuance in office of any government, were becoming political figures, whose attention to pastoral duties, even given the best intentions, had to be severely limited." "Episcopacy," *op. cit.*, p. 305. Cf. also the final paragraph on p. 308.

12. Gritsch, *op. cit.*, p. 20.

13. Cf. *The Niagara Report*, pp. 66-67, for a listing of titles in use in German territorial churches.

14. Svend Borregaard, "The Post-Reformation Developments of the Episcopacy in Denmark, Norway, and Iceland," in Asheim and Gold, editors, *op.cit.*, pp. 116-124.

15. In 1575 "the medieval ritual of episcopal consecration with anointing was used. Among the participants was Bishop Juusten of Turku about whose own earlier consecration there is no doubt. But it cannot be stated with certainty whether or not it was the intention to restore the apostolic succession through the participation of Juusten in the rite of consecration of the new bishop. Scholars are uncertain about this. Sven Kjoellerstroem for instance considers the succession definitely to have been broken during the sixteenth century. (See footnote 14, pp. 239-240.) But it is evident that during the latter part of the sixteenth century there was a clear desire to restore the traditional episcopate." Martii Parvio, "The Post-Reformation Developments of the Episcopacy in Sweden, Finland, and the Baltic States," in Asheim and Gold, editors, *op. cit.*, p. 129.

16. John Reumann, *Ministries Examined* (Minneapolis: Augsburg, 1987), pp. 140-164, especially pp. 156-157.

17. John Reumann, *Ibid.*, pp. 199-223, has a description of the debate on ministry in the process which led to the formation of the ELCA.

18. Cf. Avery Dulles and George A. Lindbeck, "Bishops and the Ministry of the Gospel," in George W. Forell and James F. McCue, editors, *Confessing One Faith* (Minneapolis: Augsburg, 1982), pp. 147-172; Robert Goeser, "The Historic Episcopate and the Lutheran Confessions," *Lutheran Quarterly*, Vol. I, No. 2 (Summer 1987), pp. 214-232; Michael Root, "The Augsburg Confession as Ecumenical Proposal: Episcopacy, Luther, and Wilhelm Maurer," *Dialog*, Vol. 28, No. 3 (Summer 1989), pp. 223-232; William Lazareth, "Evangelical Episcopate," *Lutheran Forum*, Vol. 22, No. 4 (November 1988), pp. 13-17; Robert Goeser, "Word, Ministry, and Episcopacy according to the Confessions," *op. cit.*, pp. 45-59.

19. Wilhelm Maurer, *op.cit.*, esp. pp. 59-89 and 174-236.

20. *Ibid.*, p. 81. Cf. "Address to the Christian Nobility," of 1520, LW, Vol. 44, p. 127.

21. *Ibid.*, p. 82. Cf. "The Babylonian Captivity of the Church," LW, Vol. 36, pp. 106, 111, 113.

22. *Ibid.*, p. 83. Cf. "Concerning the Ministry," LW, Vol. 40, pp. 13, 37, 40.

23. *Ibid.*, p. 84. Cf. "Instructions for the Visitors of Parish Pastors in Electoral Saxony," LW, Vol. 40, pp. 269-273. In "On War Against the Turk," of 1529, LW, Vol. 46, p. 165, Luther writes that "if the pope and the bishops were involved in the war, they would bring the greatest shame and dishonor to Christ's name because they are called to fight against the devil with the word of God and with prayer, and they would be deserting their calling and office to fight with the sword against flesh and blood."

24. *Ibid.*, p. 59.

25. LW, Vol. 34, pp. 9-61.

26. Maurer, *op.cit.*, p. 71.
27. *Ibid.*, pp. 69-70.
28. *Ibid.*, p. 79.
29. Weimar edition, Vol. 30, Part 2. Cf. the summary in Maurer, *op. cit.*, pp. 225-230.
30. Maurer, *op. cit.*, p. 228.
31. *Ibid.*, p. 80.
32. The constitution of the ELCA states, in Chapter 2, "Confession of Faith," Paragraph 2.05:

> This church accepts the Unaltered Augsburg Confession as a true witness to the Gospel, acknowledging as one with it in faith and doctrine all churches that likewise accept the teachings of the Unaltered Augsburg Confession.

and in Paragraph 2.06:

> This church accepts the other confessional writings in the Book of Concord, namely, the Apology of the Augsburg Confession, the Smalcald Articles and the Treatise, the Small Catechism, the Large Catechism, and the Formula of Concord, as further valid interpretations of the faith of the Church.

33. It is not necessary here to present a full doctrine of ministry in the Lutheran Confessions. For such a full doctrine see Arthur Carl Piepkorn, "The Sacred Ministry and Holy Ordination in the Symbolical Books of the Lutheran Church," in *Eucharist and Ministry*, Lutherans and Catholics in Dialogue IV (1970), pp. 101-119, and George A. Lindbeck, "The Lutheran Doctrine of the Ministry: Catholic and Reformed," *Theological Studies* 30:4 (December 1969), pp. 588-612. The most careful analysis of the doctrine of ministry in the Lutheran Confessions to come out of the 19th century debate on the subject is Theodosius Harnack, *Die Kirche, Ihr Amt, Ihr Regiment* (Nuremberg, 1862). Foundational for 20th century study of the Lutheran Confessions is Werner Elert, *Morphologie des Luthertums*, Vol. I (Munich: C. H. Beck Publisher, 1931), pp. 297-335. (The English translation is by Walter Hanson, *The Structure of Lutheranism*, published in St. Louis by Concordia Publishing House in 1962. See pp. 339-385 for the discussion on ministry.) Among the most widely recognized works on the Lutheran Confessions are Edmund Schlink, *Theology of the Lutheran Confessions* (first German edition, 1940) (Philadelphia: Muhlenberg Press, 1961), pp. 226-269; Friedrich Brunstaed, *Theologie der Lutherischen Bekenntnisschriften* (Guetersloh: C. Bertelsmann Verlag, 1951), pp. 114-134, 198-212; Leif Grane, *The Augsburg Confession: A Commentary* (first published in 1959) (Minneapolis: Augsburg, 1987), pp. 151-158; Holsten Fagerberg, *A New Look at the Lutheran Confessions* (first published in Sweden in the 1960s) (St. Louis: Concordia Publishing House, 1972), pp. 226-250; and Eric Gritsch and Robert Jenson, *Lutheranism: The Theological Movement and Its Confessional Writings* (Philadelphia: Fortress Press, 1976), pp. 110-123.
34. Cf. George Lindbeck, "Episcopacy," in *Promoting Unity, op. cit.*, pp. 52-53. Lindbeck states, "All three of these elements of traditional episcopal polity (viz., that there be individual persons specially charged with oversight, and they be ordaining and ordained) are more than *adiaphora*, more than matters of indifference. Other things being equal, they are positively desirable. The statement of the *Apology* regarding 'our deep desire to maintain the church polity' should be interpreted as an expression of theological principle rather than as a historically outworn response to sixteenth century circumstances."
35. E.g., *Lutheran-Episcopal Dialogue* (LED II), p. 35; and *Lutherans and Catholics in Dialogue*, Vol. IV ("Eucharist and Ministry"), pp. 106-107, 110.
36. All quotations from the Lutheran Confessional Documents are from *The Book of Concord*, edited by Theodore G. Tappert (Philadelphia, Muhlenberg Press, 1959). The sources are identified in parentheses in the text by the initials of the documents (CA for the Augsburg Confession, Apol. for the Apology of the Augsburg Confession, SA for the Smalcald Articles of 1537, and TR for the Treatise on the Power and Primacy of the Pope), followed by the number of the article in Latin numerals (where applicable) and the number of the paragraph in arabic numerals. Because the trans-

lation is from 1959 there is no attention to the use of gender-inclusive language. Because both the Latin and the German texts of the Augsburg Confession are equally official, the Tappert edition translates both, the German text at the top of each page, the Latin text below it. The letter "G" will indicate that the translation of the German text is being quoted. The letter "L" will indicate that the translation of the Latin text is being quoted. The critical edition of the texts of the Lutheran confessional writings is *Die Bekenntnisschriften der evangelisch-lutherischen Kirche*, 2nd edition (Goettingen: Vandenhoeck and Ruprecht, 1952).

37. Herbert Immenkoetter, *Der Reichstag zu Augsburg und die Confutatio* (Muenster: Aschendorf, 1979), p. 59.

38. Maurer, *op. cit.*, pp. 188-204, esp. pp. 191-197.

39. This translation follows the official German text of the Augsburg Confession which reads simply, "Derhalben ist da bishoflich Ambt nach gottlichen Rechten das Evangelium predigen," etc. The official Latin text contains a slight variation: "Proinde secundum evangelium seu, ut loquuntur, de jure divino haec iurisdictio competit episcopis ut episcopis," etc. J. Michael Miller, *The Divine Right of the Papacy in Recent Ecumenical Theology* (Analecta Gregoriana Vol. 218; Rome, Universita Gregoriana Editrice, 1980), Part II, pp. 69-134, shows that both Lutherans and Anglicans have a similar concept of "divine right."

40. Walter Kasper gives additional citations from Irenaeus and Augustine up to Thomas Aquinas which state not only that individual bishops can repudiate the *traditio* and therefore fall from the *communio*, but also that one does not owe them obedience. "Therefore, the ancient and the medieval church know repeated instances of the deposition and condemnation of bishops and even popes. There are instances of whole synods teaching heterodoxy and whose teaching is therefore not to be received. There are times when it is not the bishops, but the faithful, who hand on the true faith." (Unofficial translation from the German original, p. 337) Cf. Walter Kasper, "Die apostolische Sukzession als oekumenisches Problem," *Lehrverurteilungen—Kirchentrennend?* III. Materialien zur Lehre von den Sakramenten und vom kirchlichen Amt. (Freiburg: Herder Verlag, 1990), pp. 329-349, especially p. 337.

41. Grane, *The Augsburg Confession, op.cit.*, p. 152: "The perspective applied here to the division in the church is worthy of note, because it was the perspective of the reformers as a whole. True, the formulation of the CA is shaped by the church-political situation in 1530 in many ways, but its general aim — to demonstrate that the Lutheran Reformation has nothing to do with the formation of a new church, but is the result of the hierarchy's falling away — has nothing to do with church political tactics." Cf. also pp. 157-158, where Grane concludes: "Precisely because the Lutheran reformers do not consider themselves church founders, it is logical that the AC regards the office of bishop as being normal in the church."

42. Cf. Maurer, *op.cit.*, pp. 194-195: "Commitment to tradition, however, does not prevent rejection of ordination as a sacrament nor openness to new legal forms for the call and ordering of the office. Luther, as we have already seen in his Confession of 1528, recognized a threefold preaching office. He did not simply equate the office of bishop with that of pastor; instead, he allowed the higher office of oversight (*antistites*) to continue. Its incumbents are 'to oversee all offices, so that the teachers exercise their office and do not neglect it, the deacons distribute goods properly and do not become weary; to punish sinners and invoke the ban promptly so that every office is conducted rightly.'

"Luther's renewal of the diaconate is little known and did not last long in Lutheranism. The reason doubtless lies in the fact that CA 14 does not mention this office or a call to it . . . . He himself had a clear picture of the ancient church's practice: the deacon is, as servant of the bishop, likewise servant of the congregation. . . .

"Occasional statements of Luther then, indicate that he adopted the traditional threefold division of the pastoral office . . . . One thing is clear: these offices derived from the pastoral office—the bishop on a higher level and the preacher on a lower one—serve the truth and the effectiveness of the gospel."

43. See the extensive bibliography in Gert Haendler, *Luther on Ministerial Office and Congregational Function* (Philadelphia: Fortress Press, 1981), pp. 103-110.
44. *Lutherans and Catholics in Dialogue*, Vol. IV, "Eucharist and Ministry," p. 25.
45. The information comes from the introduction to the Treatise in the *Book of Concord*, p. 319. Cf. *Die Bekenntnisschriften der evangelisch-lutherischen Kirche*, p. XXVI.
46. That is, before the Religious Peace of Augsburg of 1555.
47. Walter Kasper, *op.cit.*, p. 339, points out that in Cologne (and there were similar occurrences elsewhere) more than one archbishop had not been consecrated bishop at all. Further, there are numerous instances in the Middle Ages of individual priests who received from popes the authority to ordain.
48. The church "is the mother that begets and bears every Christian through the Word of God," Martin Luther, Large Catechism, Creed, Par. 42.
49. Cf. Lindbeck, "The Lutheran Doctrine of the Ministry: Catholic and Reformed," *op.cit.*, pp. 593-594. Article XXI of the Augsburg Confession concludes: "This is about the sum of our teaching. As can be seen, there is nothing here that departs from the scriptures or the catholic church or the church of Rome, insofar as the ancient church is known to us from its writers." Cf. the Evangelical Lutheran Church in America's provisional statement on "Ecumenism" and its definition of "catholic": "To be *catholic* means to be committed to the fullness of the apostolic faith and its credal, doctrinal articulation for the entire world (Rom. 10:8b-15, 18b; Mark 13:10; Matt. 28:19-20). This word 'catholic' declares that the church is a community, rooted in the Christ event, extending through all places and time. It acknowledges that God has gathered a people, and continues to do so, into a community made holy in the Gospel, which it receives and proclaims. This community, a people under Christ, shares the catholic faith in the Triune God, honors and relies upon the Holy Scriptures as authoritative source and norm of the church's proclamation, receives Holy Baptism and celebrates the Lord's Supper, includes an ordained ministry and professes one, holy, catholic and apostolic Church." *A Commentary on "Ecumenism: The Vision of the ELCA," op. cit.*, p.66.
50. LED I, p. 21.
51. LED I, p. 22.
52. LED I, p. 136. See page 15, footnote 25.
53. "Pullach Report," Par. 89, quoted in LED I, p. 162.
54. LED I, p. 173.
55. LED II, p. 63.
56. ALERC Report, 1982, Par. 43, quoted in Norgren, *What Can We Share?*, p. 70.
57. "The Historic Episcopate," published by the Division of Theological Studies, Lutheran Council in the USA, 1984, p. 7.
58. *Ibid.*, p. 10.
59. These positive responses are contained in the response of the American Lutheran Church to BEM published in Max Thurian, editor, *Churches Respond to BEM*, Vol. II (Geneva: World Council of Churches, 1986), pp. 80-84. It should also be added that the response of the Standing Committee on Inter-Church Relations of the American Lutheran Church, adopted by the Church Council of the American Lutheran Church, was generally critical of BEM's advocacy of the threefold ministry of bishop, presbyter, and deacon. Cf. Michael Root, "'Do Not Grow Weary in Well-Doing': Lutheran Responses to the BEM Ministry Document," *Dialog*, Vol. 27, No. 1 (Winter 1988), pp. 23-30. Root concludes (p. 29):

> As the survey conducted here should make clear, to affirm the agenda-setting function of BEM is not to deny the significant problems in its Ministry text. Nevertheless, simply to reject the BEM Ministry text is to reject the mainstream of Lutheran ecumenism around the world. The Lutheran judgment is that this text provides the appropriate springboard for the continuing ecumenical discussion of ministry.

Cf. also Michael Seils, *Lutheran Convergence?*, LWF Report No. 25, September 1988, which is "an analysis of the Lutheran responses to the convergence document

Baptism, Eucharist and Ministry."

60. In addition to affirming the same features of BEM as those previously ascribed to the response of the American Lutheran Church, the response of the Lutheran Church in America affirms the features listed subsequently. They are cited in Max Thurian, editor, *Churches Respond to BEM*, Vol. I (Geneva: World Council of Churches, 1986), pp. 33-37. The response of the Lutheran Church in America is open to BEM's advocacy of the threefold ministry of bishop, presbyter, and deacon.

61. Note Paras. 25, 38, and 53 of Section III, "Ministry," in *Baptism, Eucharist and Ministry*.

62. Constitution of the Evangelical Lutheran Church in America, 10.11.A87.

Chapter 4: The Episcopal Church and the Ministry of the Historic Episcopate

1. G. R. Elton, *The Tudor Constitution* (Cambridge: University Press, 1960), p. 350.

2. Cf. Paul F. Bradshaw, *op. cit.*, Chapter 2.

3. "A Declaration of the Queen's Proceedings Since Her Reign," in W. E. Collins, *Queen Elizabeth's Defence of Her Proceedings in Church and State* (London: S.P.C.K., 1958), p. 45.

4. Cf. Richard Spielmann, "The Beginning of Clerical Marriage in the English Reformation: the Reigns of Edward and Mary," *Anglican and Episcopal History*, Vol. 56, No. 3 (September 1987), pp. 251-263.

5. F. D. Price, "Gloucester Diocese under Bishop Hooper," *Transactions of the Bristol and Gloucester Archeological Society* 60:51-151.

6. Cited in J. Booty, *John Jewel as Apologist of the Church of England* (London: S.P.C.K., 1963), p. 23.

7. Cf. P. M. Dawley, *John Whitgift and the English Reformation* (New York: Charles Scribner's Sons, 1954), pp. 140ff.

8. Richard Hooker, *Ecclesiastical Polity*, Book VII, chapter xiv, 11: *The Works of that Learned and Judicious Divine, Mr. Richard Hooker*, ed. John Keble, sixth edition, Vol. III, pp. 231-232; punctuation modernized.

9. Cited in Leland H. Carlson, *Martin Marprelate, Gentleman: Master Job Throckmorton Laid Open in His Colors* (San Marino: Huntington Library, 1981), p. 9.

10. W. D. J. Cargill Thompson, "The Philosopher of the 'Politic Society': Richard Hooker as a Political Thinker," in *Studies in Richard Hooker*, ed W. Speed Hill (Cleveland and London: Case Western Reserve University, 1972), p. 57.

11. Cf. especially LED II, *op. cit.*, p. 42, note 1; also Norman Sykes, *op. cit.*, and Richard Norris, "Episcopacy," *op. cit.*, pp. 304-305.

12. Manuscripts of these patristic texts, which had been lost to the medieval Western church, were rediscovered in the 17th century and led to authoritative editions in England: The First Epistle of Clement (1633), and the Letters of Ignatius of Antioch (1644, 1672).

13. Norris, "Episcopacy," *op. cit.*, p. 305.

14. Desmond Bowen, *The Idea of the Victorian Church: A Study of the Church of England, 1830-1889* (Montreal: McGill University Press, 1968), p. 51 and see p. 87 (citing Tract 1). Also E. R. Fairweather, *The Oxford Movement* (New York: Oxford University Press, 1964), pp. 55-59.

15. Frederick Denison Maurice, *The Kingdom of Christ* (1838; reprinted London: S.C.M. Press, 1958, ed A. R. Vidler), Vol. II, p. 106.

16. Maurice's view as summarized in B. M. G. Reardon, *From Coleridge to Gore: A Century of Religious Thought in Britain* (London: Longman, 1971), pp. 180-181.

17. Cf. Frederick V. Mills, Sr., *Bishops by Ballot: An Eighteenth Century Ecclesiastical Revolution* (New York: Oxford University Press, 1978).

18. Robert Goeser and William H. Petersen, *Traditions Transplanted: The Story of Anglican and Lutheran Churches in America* (Cincinnati: Forward Movement Publications, 1981), p. 36.

19. Book of Common Prayer (U.S.A., 1979), p. 877.
20. *Conference of Bishops of the Anglican Communion holden at Lambeth Palace, July 5 to August 7, 1920* (London: S.P.C.K., 1920), pp. 27-28.
21. *Ibid.*, p. 28.
22. *Ibid.*, p. 28-29.
23. *Journal of the General Convention, 1979*, p. C-46. Cf. J. Robert Wright, editor, *A Communion of Communions: One Eucharistic Fellowship* (New York: Seabury Press, 1979), pp. 3-29, and especially pp. 23-24 for application to Lutheran-Episcopal dialogue, and pp. 185-211 for the essay on "The Concordat Relationships."
24. *The COCU Consensus: In Quest of a Church of Christ Uniting*, edited by Gerald F. Moede (1984), pp. 48-50.
25. *God's Reign & Our Unity*: The Report of the Anglican-Reformed International Commission 1984 (London: S.P.C.K., 1984), p. 57, Par. 90.
26. See Chapter II, Paragraph 19, above for the full text of this section of the report.
27. *Journal of the General Convention 1982*, pp. C-56 - C-57. On the Anglican understanding of apostolicity, see also *Anglican-Orthodox Dialogue: The Dublin Agreed Statement 1984* (St. Vladimir's Seminary Press, 1985), pp. 13-14.
28. Book of Common Prayer (U.S.A., 1979), p. 855 ("An Outline of the Faith").
29. *Ibid.*, p. 517. In the emphases of Irenaeus, Ignatius, and Cyprian, respectively, each of these three paragraphs is mirrored in the writings of the early church.
30. *Ibid.*, p. 521. Much of this wording is paraphrased from the earliest prayer for the ordination of a bishop, *The Apostolic Tradition* of Hippolytus, dating from the early third century.
31. *Ibid.*, p. 510.

Chapter 5: The Gift of Full Communion

1. Norgren, *What Can We Share?*, pp. 90-92.
2. *The Niagara Report*, Paras. 25-26.
3. Cf. Paras 41-59 of *The Niagara Report* for a brief survey of the history of ministerial structure in the life of the church, and "Ministry," Paras. 19-25, in *Baptism, Eucharist and Ministry* for a similar brief survey. Cf. also William H. Petersen and Robert Goeser, *Traditions Transplanted: The Story of Anglican and Lutheran Churches in America* (Cincinnati: Forward Movement Publications, 1981).
4. Norgren, *What Can We Share?*, Paras. 26-27, pp. 91-92.
5. *The Niagara Report*, Par. 94.
6. *The Truth Shall Make You Free*, p. 204.
7. Quoted in *Consensus*: A Canadian Lutheran Journal of Theology, Vol. 12, Nos. 1-2 (1986), p. 15.
8. Cf. Mary Tanner, "The Goal of Unity in Theological Dialogues Involving Anglicans," *Einheit der Kirche*, edited by Gunther Gassmann and Peder Norgaard Hojen (Frankfurt: Verlag Otto Lembeck, 1988), pp. 69-78.
9. Cf. Michael Root, "Full Communion Between Episcopalians and Lutherans in North America: What Would It Look Like?" Unpublished Paper, Lutheran-Episcopal Dialogue III, June 17-20, 1990, p. 14.
10. Michael Root, "Bishops as Points of Unity and Continuity," Unpublished Paper, Lutheran-United Methodist Dialogue, May 1986.
11. Cf. Letty M. Russell, *Household of Freedom: Authority in Feminist Theology* (Philadelphia: Westminster Press, 1987), pp. 17-25.
12. Cf. John D. Zizioulas, *Being as Communion* (St. Vladimir's Seminary Press: 1985), pp. 171-208.
13. An example of this call is the remark of St. Thomas More in *Utopia* (Baltimore: Penguin Books, 1965), p. 124, "Male priests are allowed to marry — for there's nothing to stop a woman from becoming a priest." It should also be noted that More wrote *Utopia* in 1516, before the controversies of the Reformation broke out. He later

modified his position.

14. Much of the text which follows is indebted to portions of *The Niagara Report*, Pars. 75-87.

15. *The Niagara Report*, Pars. 100-109, identifies a series of questions which can appropriately be addressed to the current form of the historic episcopate.

CONCORDAT OF AGREEMENT

BETWEEN

THE EPISCOPAL CHURCH AND

THE EVANGELICAL LUTHERAN CHURCH IN AMERICA

Preface

The Lutheran-Episcopal Dialogue, Series III, proposes this Concordat of Agreement to its sponsoring bodies for consideration and action by The General Convention of the Episcopal Church and the Churchwide Assembly of the Evangelical Lutheran Church in America in implementation of the goal mandated by The Lutheran-Episcopal Agreement of 1982. That agreement identified the goal as "full communion (*communio in sacris*/altar and pulpit fellowship)."[1] As the meaning of "full communion" for purposes of this Concordat of Agreement both churches endorse in principle the definitions agreed to by the (international) Anglican-Lutheran Joint Working Group at Cold Ash, Berkshire, England, in 1983,[2] which they deem to be in full accord with their own definitions given in the Evangelical Lutheran Church in America's working document, "Ecumenism: The Vision of the ELCA" (1989), and given in the "Declaration on Unity" of the Episcopal Church, General Convention of 1979. During the process of consideration of this Concordat of Agreement it is expected that our churches will consult with sister churches in our respective communions (through, for example, the Anglican Consultative Council and the Lutheran World Federation) as well as those with whom we are currently engaged in dialogue.

Concordat of Agreement

1. The Episcopal Church hereby agrees that in its General Convention, and the Evangelical Lutheran Church in America hereby agrees that in its Churchwide Assembly, there shall be one vote to accept or reject, as a matter of verbal content as well as in principle, and without separate amendment, the full set of agreements to follow. If they are adopted by both churches, each church agrees to make those legislative, canonical, constitutional, and liturgical changes that are necessary and appropriate for the full communion between the churches which these agreements are designed to implement without further vote on the Concordat of Agreement by either the General Convention or the Churchwide Assembly.

A. Actions of Both Churches

Agreement in the Doctrine of the Faith

2. The Evangelical Lutheran Church in America and the Episcopal Church hereby recognize in each other the essentials of the one catholic and apostolic faith as it is witnessed in the unaltered Augsburg Confession (CA), the Small Catechism, and The Book of Common Prayer of 1979 (including the "Episcopal Services" and "An Outline of the Faith"), and as it is summarized in part in *Implications of the Gospel* and *Toward Full Communion between the Episcopal Church and the Evangelical Lutheran Church in America*, the reports of Lutheran-Episcopal Dialogue III,[3] and as it has been examined in both the papers and fourteen official conversations of Series III.[4] Each church also promises to require its ordination candidates to study each other's basic documents.

Joint Participation in the Consecration of Bishops

3. In the course of history many and various terms have been used to describe the rite by which a person becomes a bishop. In the English language these terms include: ordaining, consecrating, ordering, making, confecting, constituting, installing.

What is involved is a setting apart with prayer and the laying-on-of-hands by other bishops of a person for the distinct ministry of bishop within the one ministry of Word and Sacrament. As a result of their agreement in faith, both churches hereby pledge themselves, beginning at the time that this agreement is accepted by the General Convention of the Episcopal Church and the Churchwide Assembly of the Evangelical Lutheran Church in America, to the common joint ordinations of all future bishops as apostolic missionaries in the historic episcopate for the sake of common mission.[5]

Each church hereby promises to invite and include on an invariable basis at least three bishops of the other church, as well as three of its own, to participate in the laying-on-of-hands at the ordination of its own bishops.[6] Such a participation is the liturgical form by which the church recognizes that the bishop serves the local or regional church through ties of collegiality and consultation whose purpose is to provide links with the universal church.[7] Inasmuch as both churches agree that a ministry of *episkope* is necessary to witness to, promote, and safeguard the unity and apostolicity of the church and its continuity in doctrine and mission across time and space,[8] this participation is understood as a call for mutual planning, consultation, and interaction in *episkope*, mission, teaching, and pastoral care as well as a liturgical expression of the full communion that is being initiated by this Concordat of Agreement. Each church understands that the bishops in this action are representatives of their own churches in fidelity to the teaching and mission of the apostles. Their participation in this way embodies the historical continuity of each bishop and the diocese or synod with the apostolic church and ministry through the ages.[9]

B. Actions of The Episcopal Church

4. In light of the agreement that the threefold ministry of bishops, presbyters, and deacons in historic succession will be the future pattern of the one ordained ministry of Word and Sacrament in both churches as they begin to live in full communion,[10] the Episcopal Church hereby recognizes now the full authenticity of the ordained ministries presently existing within the Evangelical Lutheran Church in America. The Episcopal Church acknowledges the pastors and bishops of the Evangelical Lutheran Church in America as priests within the Evangelical Lutheran Church in America and the bishops of the Evangelical Lutheran Church in America as chief pastors exercising a ministry of *episkope* over the jurisdictional areas of the

Evangelical Lutheran Church in America in which they preside.[11]

5. To enable the full communion that is coming into being by means of this Concordat of Agreement, the Episcopal Church hereby pledges, at the same time that this Concordat of Agreement is accepted by its General Convention and by the Churchwide Assembly of the Evangelical Lutheran Church in America, to begin the process for enacting a temporary suspension, in this case only, of the 17th century restriction that "no persons are allowed to exercise the offices of bishop, priest, or deacon in this Church unless they are so ordained, or have already received such ordination with the laying on of hands by bishops who are themselves duly qualified to confer Holy Orders."[12] The purpose of this action will be to permit the full interchangeability and reciprocity of all Evangelical Lutheran Church in America pastors as priests or presbyters and all Evangelical Lutheran Church in America deacons as deacons in the Episcopal Church without any further ordination or re-ordination or supplemental ordination whatsoever, subject always to canonically or constitutionally approved invitation (see pars. 14, 15, and 16 below). The purpose of temporarily suspending this restriction, which has been a constant requirement in Anglican polity since the Ordinal of 1662,[13] is precisely in order to secure the future implementation of the ordinals' same principle within the eventually fully integrated ministries. It is for this reason that the Episcopal Church can feel confident in taking this unprecedented step with regard to the Evangelical Lutheran Church in America.

6. The Episcopal Church hereby endorses the Lutheran affirmation that the historic catholic episcopate under the Word of God must always serve the gospel,[14] and that the ultimate authority under which bishops preach and teach is the gospel itself.[15] In testimony and implementation thereof, the Episcopal Church agrees to establish and welcome, either by itself or jointly with the Evangelical Lutheran Church in America, structures for collegial and periodic review of its episcopal ministry, as well as that of the Evangelical Lutheran Church in America, with a view to evaluation, adaptation, improvement, and continual reform in the service of the gospel.[16]

C. Actions of the Evangelical Lutheran Church in America

7. The Evangelical Lutheran Church in America agrees that all its

bishops will be understood as ordained, like other pastors, for life service of the gospel in the pastoral ministry of the historic episcopate,[17] even though tenure in office of the churchwide bishop and synodical bishops may be terminated by retirement, resignation, or conclusion of term however constitutionally ordered. The Evangelical Lutheran Church in America further agrees to revise its rite for the "Installation of a Bishop"[18] to reflect this understanding. In keeping with these principles the Evangelical Lutheran Church in America also agrees to revise its constitution (e.g., 16.51.41.) so that all bishops, including those no longer active, shall be regular members of the Conference of Bishops.[19]

8.   As regards ordained ministry, the Evangelical Lutheran Church in America affirms, in the context of its confessional heritage, the teaching of the Augsburg Confession that Lutherans do not intend to depart from the historic faith and practice of catholic Christianity.[20] The Evangelical Lutheran Church in America therefore agrees to make constitutional and liturgical provision that only bishops shall ordain all clergy. Presbyters shall continue to participate in the laying-on-of-hands at all ordinations of presbyters. It is further understood that episcopal and presbyteral office in the church is to be understood and exercised as servant ministry, and not for domination or arbitrary control.[21] Appropriate liturgical expression of these understandings will be made.[22] Both churches acknowledge that the diaconate, including its place within the threefold ministerial office, is in need of continued study and reform, which they pledge themselves to undertake in consultation with one another.[23]

9.   In light of the above agreements and of the actions of the Episcopal Church, the Evangelical Lutheran Church in America hereby recognizes now the full authenticity of the ordained ministries presently existing within the Episcopal Church, acknowledging the bishops, priests, and deacons of the Episcopal Church all as pastors in their respective orders within the Episcopal Church and the bishops of the Episcopal Church as chief pastors in the historic succession exercising a ministry of *episkope* over the jurisdictional areas of the Episcopal Church in which they preside. In preparation for the full communion that is coming into being by means of this Concordat of Agreement, the Evangelical Lutheran Church in America also pledges, at the time that this Concordat of Agreement is accepted by the Churchwide Assembly of the Evangelical Lutheran Church in America and the General Convention of the Episcopal

Church, to begin the process for enacting a dispensation for ordinands of the Episcopal Church from its ordination requirement of subscription to the unaltered Augsburg Confession (Constitution of the Evangelical Lutheran Church in America 10:21) in order to permit the full interchangeability and reciprocity of all Episcopal Church bishops as bishops, of all Episcopal Church priests as pastors, and of all Episcopal Church deacons as may be determined (see Par. 8 above), within the Evangelical Lutheran Church in America without any supplemental oath or subscription, subject always to canonically or constitutionally approved invitation (see Pars. 14, 15, and 16 below). The purpose of this dispensation, which heretofore has not been made by the Evangelical Lutheran Church in America for the clergy of any other church, is precisely in order to serve the future implementation, in the full communion that will follow, of the agreement in the doctrine of the faith identified in Paragraph 2 (above) of this Concordat of Agreement.

D. Actions of Both Churches

Joint Commission

10. Both churches hereby authorize the establishment of a joint ecumenical/doctrinal/liturgical commission to moderate the details of these changes, to assist joint planning for mission, to facilitate consultation and common decision making through appropriate channels in fundamental matters that the churches may face together in the future, to enable the process of new consecrations/ordinations of bishops in both churches as they occur, and to issue guidelines as requested and as may seem appropriate. It will prepare a national service that will celebrate the inauguration of this Concordat of Agreement as a common obedience to Christ in mission. At this service the mutual recognition of faith will be celebrated and, if possible, new bishops from each church will be consecrated/ordained for the synods or dioceses that have elected them, initiating the provisions hereby agreed upon.

Wider Context

11. In thus moving to establish one ordained ministry in geographically overlapping episcopates, open to women as well as to men, to married persons as well as to single persons, both churches agree that the historic catholic episcopate, which they embrace, can be locally

adapted and reformed in the service of the gospel. In this spirit they offer this Concordat of Agreement and growth toward full communion for serious consideration among the churches of the Reformation as well as among the Orthodox and Roman Catholic churches. They pledge widespread consultation during the process at all stages. Each church promises to issue no official commentary on this text that has not been approved by the joint commission as a legitimate interpretation thereof.

Existing Relationships

12. Each church agrees that the other church will continue to live in communion with all the churches with whom the latter is now in communion. Each church also pledges prior consultation about this Concordat of Agreement with those churches. The Evangelical Lutheran Church in America continues to be in full communion (pulpit and altar fellowship) with all member churches of the Lutheran World Federation. This Concordat of Agreement with the Episcopal Church does not imply or inaugurate any automatic communion between the Episcopal Church and the other member churches of the Lutheran World Federation. The Episcopal Church continues to be in full communion with all of the provinces of the Anglican Communion, and with Old Catholic Churches of Europe, with the united churches of the Indian sub-continent, with the Mar Thoma Church, and with the Philippine Independent Church. This Concordat of Agreement with the Evangelical Lutheran Church in America does not imply or inaugurate any automatic communion between the Evangelical Lutheran Church in America and the other provinces of the Anglican Communion or any other churches with whom the Episcopal Church is in full communion.

Other Dialogues

13. Both churches agree that each will continue to engage in dialogue with other churches and traditions. Both churches agree to take each other and this Concordat of Agreement into account at every stage in their dialogues with other churches and traditions. Where appropriate, both churches will seek to engage in joint dialogues. On the basis of this Concordat of Agreement, both churches pledge that they will not enter into formal agreements with other churches and traditions without prior consultation with each other. At the same time both

churches pledge that they will not impede the development of relationships and agreements with other churches and traditions with whom they have been in dialogue.

E. FULL COMMUNION

14. Of all the historical processes involved in realizing full communion between the Episcopal Church and the Evangelical Lutheran Church in America, the achieving of full interchangeability of ordained ministries will probably take longest. While the two churches will fully acknowledge the authenticity of each other's ordained ministries from the beginning of the process, the creation of a common, and therefore fully interchangeable, ministry will occur with the full incorporation of all active bishops in the historic episcopate by common joint ordinations and the continuing process of collegial consultation in matters of Christian faith and life. Full communion will also include the activities of the joint commission (Par. 10 above), as well as the establishment of "recognized organs of regular consultation and communication, including episcopal collegiality, to express and strengthen the fellowship and enable common witness, life and service."[24] Thereby the churches are permanently committed to common mission and ministry on the basis of agreement in faith, recognizing each other fully as churches in which the gospel is preached and the holy Sacraments administered. All provisions specified above will continue in effect.

15. On the basis of this Concordat of Agreement, at a given date recommended by the joint commission, the Evangelical Lutheran Church in America and the Episcopal Church will announce the completion of the process by which they enjoy full communion with each other. They will share one ordained ministry in two churches that are in full communion, still autonomous in structure yet interdependent in doctrine, mission, and ministry.

16. Consequent to the acknowledgment of full communion and respecting always the internal discipline of each church, both churches now accept in principle the full interchangeability and reciprocity of their ordained ministries, recognizing bishops as bishops, pastors as priests and presbyters and *vice versa*, and deacons as deacons. In consequence of our mutual pledge to a future already anticipated in Christ and the church of the early centuries,[25] each church will make such necessary revisions of canons and constitution so that ordained

clergy can, upon canonically or constitutionally approved invitation, function as clergy in corresponding situations within either church. The churches will authorize such celebrations of the Eucharist as will accord full recognition to each other's episcopal ministries and sacramental services. All further necessary legislative, canonical, constitutional, and liturgical changes will be coordinated by the joint ecumenical/doctrinal/liturgical commission hereby established.

Conclusion

We receive with thanksgiving the gift of unity which is already given in Christ.

> He is the image of the invisible God, the first-born of all creation; for in him all things were created, in heaven and on earth, visible and invisible, whether thrones or dominions or principalities or authorities — all things were created through him and for him. He is before all things, and in him all things hold together. He is the head of the body, the church; he is the beginning, the first-born from the dead, that in everything he might be pre-eminent. For in him all the fulness of God was pleased to dwell, and through him to reconcile to himself all things, whether on earth or in heaven, making peace by the blood of his cross. Col. 1:15-20
>
> Repeatedly Christians have confessed that the unity of the church is given, not achieved. The church can only be one because it is constituted by the gospel in word and sacrament, and there is but one gospel. What Christians are seeking when they engage in the tasks and efforts associated with ecumenism is to discover how the unity they have already been given by the gospel can be manifested faithfully in terms of the church's mission.[26]

We do not know to what new, recovered, or continuing tasks of mission this proposed Concordat of Agreement will lead our churches, but we give thanks to God for leading us to this point. We entrust ourselves to that leading in the future, confident that our full communion will be a witness to the gift and goal already present in Christ,

105

"that God may be everything to every one" (I Cor. 15:28). It is the gift of Christ that we are sent as he has been sent (John 17:17-26), that our unity will be received and perceived as we participate in the mission of the Son in obedience to the Father through the power and presence of the Holy Spirit.[27]

> Now to the one who by the power at work within us is able to do far more abundantly than all that we ask or think, to God be glory in the church and in Christ Jesus to all generations, for ever and ever. Amen. (Eph. 3:20-21)

The Epiphany of Our Lord
January 6, 1991

Notes

1 Cf. the complete text of the 1982 Agreement in paragraph 1 of the report *Toward Full Communion* which accompanies this proposed Concordat of Agreement.

2. *Anglican-Lutheran Relations: Report of the Anglican-Lutheran Joint Working Group, Cold Ash, Berkshire, England—1983*, in William A. Norgren, *What Can We Share?* (Cincinnati, Forward Movement Publications, 1985), pp. 90-92. The relevant portion of the report reads as follows:

> By full communion we here understand a relationship between two distinct churches or communions. Each maintains its own autonomy and recognizes the catholicity and apostolicity of the other, and each believes the other to hold the essentials of the Christian faith:
>
> > a) subject to such safeguards as ecclesial discipline may properly require, members of one body may receive the sacraments of the other;
> >
> > b) subject to local invitation, bishops of one church may take part in the consecration of the bishops of the other, thus acknowledging the duty of mutual care and concern;
> >
> > c) subject to church regulation, a bishop, pastor/priest or deacon of one ecclesial body may exercise liturgical functions in a congregation of the other body if invited to do so and also, when requested, pastoral care of the other's members;
> >
> > d) it is also a necessary addition and complement that there should be recognized organs of regular consultation and communication, including episcopal collegiality, to express and strengthen the fellowship and enable common witness, life and service.
>
> To be in full communion means that churches become interdependent while remaining autonomous. One is not elevated to be the judge of the other nor can it remain insensitive to the other; neither is each body committed to every secondary feature of the tradition of the other. Thus the corporate strength of the churches is enhanced in love, and an isolated independence is restrained.
>
> Full communion should not imply the suppressing of ethnic, cultural or ecclesial characteristics of traditions which may in fact be maintained and developed by diverse institutions within one communion.

3. Cf. the working document, "Ecumenism: The Vision of the Evangelical Lutheran Church in America," D,1 and 2, adopted by the Evangelical Lutheran Church in America on August 25, 1989, "to offer provisional and interim guidance for this church during the 1990-1991 biennium"; and the "Declaration on Unity" adopted by the 1979 General Convention of the Episcopal Church.

4. Lutheran-Episcopal Dialogue III has held the following meetings, with the papers presented and discussed listed under each meeting:

> 1) December 4-7, 1983, Techny, Illinois
> Walter R. Bouman, "Lutheran Analysis and Critique of *The Final Report* of the Anglican-Roman Catholic International Commission (ARCIC)"
> J. Robert Wright, "Anglican Analysis and Critique of *The Ministry in the Church* (report of the international Roman Catholic/Lutheran Joint

Commission), as well as of the concept of 'bishop' in the *Book of Concord*"

2) June 10-13, 1984, New York, New York
William H. Petersen, "Implications of the Gospel"
Walter R. Bouman, "The Gospel and Its Implications"
L. William Countryman, "The Gospel and the Institutions of the Church with Particular Reference to the Historic Episcopate"
Robert J. Goeser, "Augustana 28 and Lambeth 4: Episcopacy as Adiaphoron or Necessity"
Joseph A. Burgess, "Teaching Authority in the Lutheran Tradition"
John H. Rodgers, Jr., "Teaching Authority in the Church: The Gospel, the Church, and the Role of Bishops — Some Anglican Reflections"
William A. Norgren, "The Way to Full Communion"
J. Robert Wright, "Lutherans and Episcopalians: The Way Forward"
William G. Rusch, "Mutual Recognition of Ministries"

3) January 27-30, 1985, Techny, Illinois
Marianne H. Micks, "Mission and Prayer"
Paul Berge, "A Response to Bill Countryman's paper, 'The Gospel and the Institutions of the Church'"
Wayne Weissenbuehler, "Critical Questions and a Few Reflections on the paper *Implications of the Gospel* by the Rev. Dr. William H. Petersen"
Marianne H. Micks, "Questions Arising from Walter Bouman's Paper, 'The Gospel and Its Implications'"
Mark Dyer, "Some Questions for Dr. Goeser Concerning Augustana 28 and Lambeth 4: Episcopacy as Adiaphoron or Necessity"

4) June 2-5, 1985, Erlanger, Kentucky
Jerald C. Brauer, "Bishops and the Lutherans in the United States"

5) January 26-29, 1986, Techny, Illinois
William G. Rusch, "Towards Full Communion"
J. Robert Wright, "Some Initial Reactions to the Paper of William Rusch"
Roland Foster, "The Development of Episcopacy in the American Episcopal Church"
Jerald C. Joersz, "Altar and Pulpit Fellowship: LCMS' Model for External Unity in the Church"
L. William Countryman, "Discussion Questions on 'Teaching Authority in the Lutheran Tradition,' by Joseph A. Burgess"
Walter R. Bouman, "Questions on John Rodgers' 'Teaching Authority in the Church'"

6) June 8-11, 1986, Cincinnati, Ohio
J. Robert Wright, "Anglican/Episcopal Recognition of the Augsburg Confession—An Actual Possibility"
John H. Rodgers, Jr., "A Comparison of the Catechisms of Lutheran and Episcopal Churches"
Walter R. Bouman, "Lutheran Recognition of the Book of Common Prayer"
Robert Goeser, "The Word of God According to Luther and the Confessions"
Marianne H. Micks, "The Doctrine of the Church in Anglican Thought"

7) January 11-14, 1987, Techny, Illinois
Discussion of "The Gospel and Its Implications"

8) June 7-11, 1987, Techny, Illinois
Paul Berge, "The Gospel and Its Implications in Galatians, The Augsburg

108

Confession, and the Thirty-Nine Articles"
Discussion of *Implications of the Gospel*

9) January 3-6, 1988, Techny, Illinois
Walter R. Bouman, "Report on the Niagara Falls Consultation on *Episkope* and the Proposed *Niagara Report*"
William G. Rusch, "Recognition and Reception as Ecumenical Concepts"
William A. Norgren, "Relations Between the Churches of England and Sweden, with Special Emphasis on Recognition of Faith"
Discussion and Final Adoption of *Implications of the Gospel*

10) January 5-8, 1989, Delray Beach, Florida
Samuel Nafzger, "Hopes and Expectations of the Lutheran Church— Missouri Synod in Ecumenical Dialogue"
Robert Goeser, "The Augsburg Confession in the Life of the Lutheran Church"
William A. Norgren, "Ecclesial Recognition"
William G. Rusch, "Some Comments on Recognition by Lutheran Churches"

11) June 4-7, 1989, Burlingame, California
L. William Countryman, "The Historic Episcopate: Further Reflections"
John Booty, "The Place of the Book of Common Prayer in Anglicanism"
Paul Erickson, "The Place of Luther's Small Catechism in Lutheranism"
Paul Berge, "Niagara Recommendations from a Lutheran Point of View"
James Griffiss, "Niagara Recommendations from an Anglican Point of View"

12) January 4-7, 1990, Delray Beach, Florida
Richard Norris, "Bishops and the Mutual Recognition and Reconciliation of Ministries"
Discussion of the LED III Report, *Toward Full Communion Between the Episcopal Church and Evangelical Lutheran Church in America*, and the proposed Agreement

13) June 17-20, 1990, New Orleans, Louisiana
Michael Root, "Full Communion Between Episcopalians and Lutherans: What Would it Look Like?"
J. Robert Wright, "Response to the Paper by Michael Root"
Eric W. Gritsch, "Episcopacy: The Legacy of the Lutheran Confessions"
Sir Henry Chadwick, "Response to the Paper by Eric Gritsch"
John H. P. Reumann, "Report on the Work of the Evangelical Lutheran Church in America's Task Force on the Study of Ministry with Special Reference to the work of Lutheran-Episcopal Dialogue III"
Discussion of the LED III Report, *Toward Full Communion Between the Episcopal Church and the Evangelical Lutheran Church in America*, and the proposed Agreement

14) January 3-6, 1991, Delray Beach, Florida
Robert Jenson, "The Episcopate as 'Sign' in Ecumenical Dialogue"
Discussion of and final action on the LED III Report, *Toward Full Communion Between the Episcopal Church and the Evangelical Lutheran Church in America*, and the proposed "Concordat of Agreement"

5. Cf. Richard Grein, "The Bishop as Chief Missionary," in Charles R. Henery, editor, *Beyond the Horizon: Frontiers for Mission* (Cincinnati: Forward Movement Publications, 1986), pp. 64-80.

6. *The Niagara Report* (London: Church House Publishing, 1988), Pars. 91 and 96; The Council of Nicaea, Canon 4.

7. Michael Root, "Full Communion Between Episcopalians and Lutherans in North America: What Would It Look Like?" (Unpublished Paper, LED III, June 1990), pp. 10-16. Cf. Michael Root, "Bishops as Points of Unity and Continuity" (Unpublished Paper, Lutheran-United Methodist Dialogue, May 1986).

8. *The Niagara Report*, Par. 69; The Pullach Report, Par. 79; The Lutheran-United Methodist Common Statement on Episcopacy, Par. 28.

9. Cf. Resolutions of the 1979 and 1985 General Conventions of the Episcopal Church, The Canterbury Statement, Par. 16, of the Anglican-Roman Catholic International Commission, and the Evangelical Lutheran Church in America's provisional statement, "Ecumenism: The Vision of the Evangelical Lutheran Church in America," D,3.

10. Chicago-Lambeth Quadrilateral 4.

11. *The Niagara Report*, Par. 94. Cf. Raymond E. Brown, *Priest and Bishop: Biblical Reflections* (New York: Paulist Press, 1970), pp. 83-85.

12. Preface to the Ordinal, The Book of Common Prayer, p. 510.

13. Cf. *The Study of Anglicanism*, ed. Stephen Sykes and John Booty (London/Philadelphia: SPCK/Fortress, 1988), pp. 149, 151, 238, 290, 304-305; Paul F. Bradshaw, *The Anglican Ordinal* (London: SPCK, 1971), Chapter 6.

14. *The Niagara Report*, Par. 91, Augsburg Confession Article 7, Article 28.

15. Cf. Joseph A. Burgess, "An Evangelical Episcopate," in Todd Nichol and Marc Kolden, editors, *Called and Ordained* (Minneapolis: Fortress Press, 1990), p. 147.

16. Cf. *The Niagara Report*, Pars. 90, 95, and especially 100-110 as examples of the questions and concerns involved in such evaluation. Cf. also *Baptism, Eucharist and Ministry*, Ministry Par. 38.

17. Cf. *The Niagara Report*, Par. 90.

18. *Occasional Services* (Minneapolis: Augsburg Publishing House, 1982), pp. 218-223.

19. We understand the term "regular" to mean "according to constitutionally regulated provisions." A revised constitution of the Evangelical Lutheran Church in America may, for example, give voice but not vote in the Conference of Bishops to bishops who are no longer actively functioning in the office of bishop by reason of retirement, resignation to accept another call, or conclusion of term.

20. Augsburg Confession, Article 21 (Tappert, page 47); cf. Treatise on the Power and Primacy of the Pope, Par. 66 (Tappert, p. 331).

21. Cf. II Cor. 10:8; also *Anglican-Orthodox Dialogue: The Dublin Agreed Statement 1984* (St. Vladimir's Seminary Press, 1985), pp. 13-14, and *ARCIC, The Final Report* (London: SPCK and Catholic Truth Society, 1982), pp. 83 and 89.

22. Cf. *The Niagara Report*, Par. 92.

23. *Baptism, Eucharist and Ministry*, Ministry Par. 24. Cf. James M. Barnett, *The Diaconate: A Full and Equal Order* (New York: The Seabury Press, 1981), pp. 133-197; John E. Booty, *The Servant Church: Diaconal Ministry and the Episcopal Church* (Wilton, CT, Morehouse-Barlow, 1982); and J. Robert Wright, "The Emergence of the Diaconate: Biblical and Patristic Sources," *Liturgy*, Vol. 2, No. 4 (Fall 1982), pp. 17-23, 67-71.

24. The Cold Ash report, par. d. See footnote 2, above.

25. Cf. John D. Zizioulas, *Being as Communion* (New York: St. Vladimir's Seminary Press, 1985), pp. 171-208.

26. *Implications of the Gospel*, Par. 98.

27. *The Niagara Report*, Pars. 25-26.

THE DISSENTING REPORT
OF LUTHERAN-EPISCOPAL DIALOGUE, SERIES III

The undersigned have voted against the report "Toward Full Communion Between the Episcopal Church and the Evangelical Lutheran Church in America" and the proposed "Concordat of Agreement."

We believe that Scripture and the Augsburg Confession clearly teach that the Word of God rightly preached and rightly administered in the sacraments of Baptism and the Lord's Supper constitutes the sole and sufficient basis for the true unity of the Christian church. This unity Lutherans and Episcopalians already share in Christ. In this "Concordat," however, the historic episcopate is made to be a necessity for church fellowship and thus essential to the unity of the church. Under the terms of this "Concordat," the process toward "full communion" will thus not be realized until there is complete interchangeability of ordained ministries on the basis of the joint ordination of all active bishops of the ELCA—ordained as bishops after the acceptance of this "Concordat"—into the historic episcopacy through the Anglican succession. We believe such provisions for the ministry of the church belong to the realm of the *adiaphora* (things often important but never essential to the unity of the church). To introduce the historic episcopate into the ELCA under the terms of this "Concordat" is to make an *adiaphoron* into a matter of necessity.

We believe that the present context calls for a clear witness to the central insights of the Reformation and a commitment to unassuming servanthood on behalf of Christ's mission in the world. We believe that Christian ecumenism best serves the apostolic mission of the church when it provides for the speaking of God's Word and the administration of the Sacraments in a multitude of ways appropriate to a variety of times and places.

We cherish the fellowship now existing between the Episcopal Church and the ELCA. We look forward to the maturation of this friendship and the engagement of both churches in broader ecumenical ventures as well. We believe that to introduce the historic episcopate into the

ELCA under the terms of the "Concordat" could needlessly jeopardize a treasured friendship as well as endanger the collaboration in the gospel and table fellowship we now enjoy. We believe that it could also provoke controversy and division among the congregations and ministers of the ELCA.

Robert J. Goeser
Professor of Church History
Pacific Lutheran
  Theological Seminary

Paul S. Berge
Professor of New Testament
Luther Northwestern
  Theological Seminary

THE ASSENTING REPORT
OF LUTHERAN-EPISCOPAL DIALOGUE, SERIES III

(At the concluding session of the dialogue, the participants authorized the co-chairpersons of the dialogue to release a response to the Dissenting, or Minority Report if they deemed this appropriate.)

We, the undersigned ELCA members of Lutheran-Episcopal Dialogue III, respect the right of our dissenting colleagues to *interpret* the report and the agreement for full communion as they choose. However, we cannot recognize their interpretation as correct. The initiative of the Episcopal members of the dialogue has been to recognize the existing pastoral ministry of the Evangelical Lutheran Church in America as authentic and to propose a temporary suspension of the preface to the ordinal so that pastors of the ELCA can be invited to function in place of priests of the Episcopal Church. That initiative has made it *possible*, not necessary, for us to propose simultaneously and in concert with our Episcopal colleagues the joint consecration of *future* bishops resulting in the future participation of ELCA bishops in the historic episcopal succession. In this we have simply been free to propose the restoration of the traditional polity which the Lutheran *Book of Concord* espouses (Pars. 42-47 of the Report). To be given this freedom is in no way "to make an *adiaphoron* into a matter of necessity."

We regret the fact that our colleagues could not endorse the mandate of our churches in which we were directed to move beyond present level of fellowship toward full communion. We regret the fact that they could not endorse the definition of full communion approved by the Anglican and Lutheran world communions, which calls for the bishops of one church to "take part in the consecration of the bishops of the other, thus acknowledging the duty of mutual care and concern."

We regret the fact that they no longer endorse the conclusion of the Lutheran Council in the U.S.A. report on "The Historic Episcopate," which both of them helped to formulate in 1984, and in which they stated:

When the "historic episcopate" faithfully proclaims the gospel and administers the sacraments, it may be accepted as a symbol of the church's unity and continuity throughout the centuries provided that it is not viewed as a necessity for the *validity* (our emphasis) of the church's ministry.

We regret the fact that our colleagues cannot endorse the full position of the Lutheran "Formula of Concord" on *adiaphora*, namely, that the church has the "liberty to avail itself" of elements of the tradition which it might have to resist if required of it under persecution or duress (Epitome, Article X, p. 494). Our churches are able to invite bishops to participate in each other's *future* episcopal consecrations (Concordat of Agreement, Par. 3) *because* both churches do *now* recognize the full authenticity of each other's ministries without the imposition of any demands or further conditions (Concordat of Agreement, Pars. 4 and 9).

We fully agree with our colleagues

that Christian ecumenism best serves the apostolic mission of the church when it provides for the speaking of God's Word and the administration of the Sacraments in a multitude of ways appropriate to a variety of times and places

because we support the provision of the Lambeth Quadrilateral that the historic episcopate can be "locally adapted in the methods of its administration to the varying needs of the nations and peoples called of God into the Unity of His Church" (Report, Par. 33).

We pray that the controversy and division which our colleagues fear not be incited by those who are determined in advance to resist full communion between our churches and to oppose full collegiality among our bishops.

The Rev. Dr. Paul Erickson
The Rev. Dr. Walter R. Bouman
The Rev. Dr. William G. Rusch
The Rev. Wayne E. Weissenbuehler, Bishop
The Rev. Cyril Wismar, Sr.

Statement of Lutheran Church—Missouri Synod Participants

Representatives of the Lutheran Church—Missouri Synod have been full participants in all three rounds of the Lutheran-Episcopal Dialogue. The LCMS representatives to these discussions have welcomed with appreciation this opportunity to engage in interconfessional dialogue with brothers and sisters in Christ. The Synod's participation in such discussions reflects its longstanding commitment to the biblical mandate that Christians seek to manifest externally the unity already given to them in the body of Christ and to do so on the basis of agreement in the confession of the gospel "In all its articles (FC SD X, 31)."

The Representatives of the LCMS have recognized that due to agreements reached among the other representatives of the dialogue, and in particular, the Lutheran/Episcopal Interim Sharing of the Eucharist Agreement adopted by the non-LCMS participant churches in 1982, the aim of the third round of dialogue has shifted to focus on the achieving of full communion (altar and pulpit fellowship) between the Episcopal Church and the Evangelical Lutheran Church in America. In response to a specific invitation, the LCMS has continued to send representatives as full participants in LED III, even while it has not been a part of the 1982 Agreement, nor the efforts to reach full communion. Although Missouri Synod participation has been limited by these circumstances the LCMS representatives wish to express their gratitude to all the members of the dialogue for welcoming LCMS participation in this phase of dialogue. The LCMS participants remain committed to the value of the discussions themselves as vehicles to achieve greater understanding of and agreement in "the truth as it is taught in the Scriptures and confessed in the Lutheran symbols" ("Guidelines for Participation in Ecumenical Dialogs," prepared by the Commission on Theology and Church Relations, 1975).

We, the LCMS representatives of LED III, ask our gracious God to bless the efforts of our friends and colleagues on the dialogue to achieve a common witness to the gospel of Jesus Christ. We express our best wishes to all present and past members of the dialogue and thank God for the friendships we have come to enjoy and the commonalities we share. And, we look forward to future opportunities to address together differences in doctrine and practice which continue to divide the church.

The Rev. Carl Bornmann
The Rev. Dr. Norman E. Nagel
The Rev. Jerald C. Joersz

LIST OF PARTICIPANTS

Episcopal Church, U.S.A.

The Rev. Dr. L. William Countryman The Church Divinity School of the Pacific Berkeley, California	Voted:	YES
The Rt. Rev. Mark Dyer Bishop of Bethlehem Bethlehem, Pennsylvania	Voted:	YES
The Rt. Rev. Richard F. Grein Bishop of New York New York, New York	Voted:	YES
The Rev. John R. Kevern, *secretary* Assistant, St. James Cathedral Chicago, Illinois	Voted:	YES
The Very Rev. William Petersen Dean, Bexley Hall Colgate-Rochester Divinity School Rochester, New York	Voted:	YES

The Very Rev. John H. Rodgers, Jr. Voted: YES
Director, Stanway Institute for World Mission and Evangelism
Trinity Episcopal School for Ministry
Ambridge, Pennsylvania

The Rt. Rev. William G. Weinhauer, *co-chair* Voted: YES
Bishop of Western North Carolina (retired)
Asheville, North Carolina

Staff
The Rev. Dr. William Norgren
The Ecumenical Officer
The Executive Council of the Episcopal Church
New York, New York

Consultant
The Rev. Dr. J. Robert Wright
The General Theological Seminary
New York, New York

The Evangelical Lutheran Church in America

The Rev. Dr. Paul S. Berge Luther Northwestern Theological Seminary St. Paul, Minnesota	Voted:	NO
The Rev. Dr. Walter R. Bouman Trinity Lutheran Seminary Columbus, Ohio	Voted:	YES
The Rev. Dr. Paul E. Erickson, *co-chair* Bishop (Retired), Illinois Synod of the L.C.A. Wheaton, Illinois	Voted:	YES
The Rev. Dr. Robert J. Goeser Pacific Lutheran Theological Seminary Berkeley, California	Voted:	NO
The Rev. Dr. William G. Rusch Executive Director, Office for Ecumenical Affairs Evangelical Lutheran Church in America Chicago, Illinois	Voted:	YES
The Rev. Dr. Edward D. Schneider Good Shepherd Lutheran Church Champaign, Illinois	Voted:	NO
The Rev. Wayne E. Weissenbuehler Bishop, Rocky Mountain Synod Denver, Colorado	Voted:	YES
The Rev. Cyril M. Wismar, Sr. Auxiliary Bishop (Retired) East Coast Synod/A.E.L.C. Falls Village, Connecticut	Voted:	YES

Staff
The Rev. Dr. Daniel F. Martensen
Associate Director, Office for Ecumenical Affairs
The Evangelical Lutheran Church in America
Chicago, Illinois

The Lutheran Church—Missouri Synod

The Rev. Carl Bornmann   Voted: ABSTAIN
St. John's Lutheran Church
Luxemburg, Wisconsin

The Rev. Dr. Norman E. Nagel   Voted: ABSTAIN
Concordia Theological Seminary
St. Louis, Missouri

The Rev. Jerald Joersz   Voted: ABSTAIN
Assistant Executive Director,
  Commission on Theology and Church Relations
The Lutheran Church—Missouri Synod
St. Louis, Missouri

Staff
The Rev. Dr. Samuel Nafzger
Executive Director,
  Commission on Theology and Church Relations
The Lutheran Church—Missouri Synod
St. Louis, Missouri